TEVILLE

ROUND MOUNTAIN

KINGDOM COME

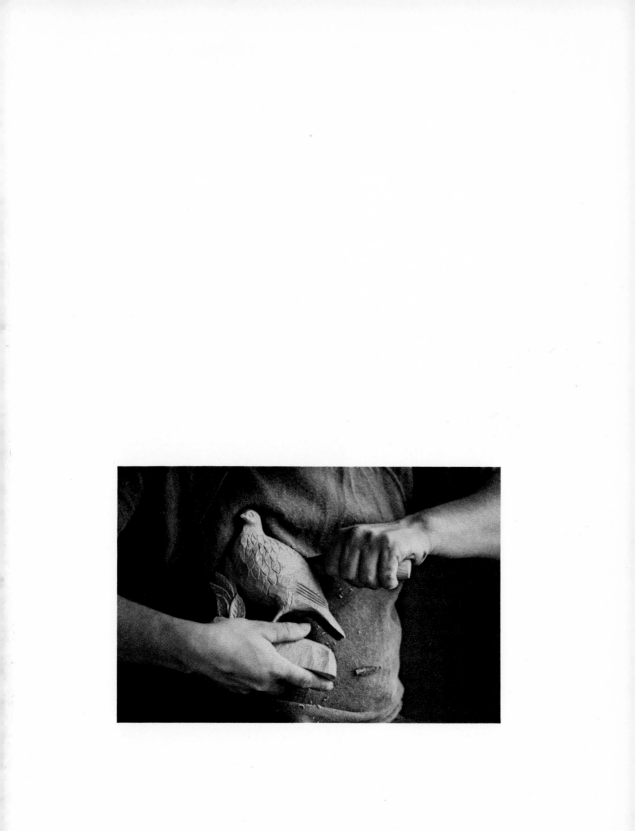

American Mountain People

Prepared by the Special Publications Division
National Geographic Society, Washington, D. C.

AMERICAN MOUNTAIN PEOPLE

Photographed by BRUCE DALE
National Geographic Photographer

Contributing Authors
CLAY ANDERSON, CHARLTON OGBURN, BILL
    PETERSON, ZEKE SCHER, STEPHEN WENNSTROM

Published by
THE NATIONAL GEOGRAPHIC SOCIETY
MELVIN M. PAYNE, *President*
MELVILLE BELL GROSVENOR, *Editor-in-Chief*
GILBERT M. GROSVENOR, *Editor*

Prepared by
THE SPECIAL PUBLICATIONS DIVISION
ROBERT L. BREEDEN, *Editor*
DONALD J. CRUMP, *Associate Editor*
PHILIP B. SILCOTT, *Senior Assistant Editor*
MERRILL WINDSOR, *Managing Editor*
TUCKER L. ETHERINGTON, LINDA LU MOORE,
    ANN CROUCH RESH, *Research*
JOHANNA G. FARREN, PEGGY D. WINSTON,
    Editorial Assistants

Illustrations

BRYAN D. HODGSON, *Picture Editor*
LINDA LU MOORE, *Historical Picture Research*
MARGERY G. DUNN, RONALD M. FISHER,
    WILLIAM R. GRAY, STRATFORD C. JONES,
    Picture Legends

Design and Art Direction

JOSEPH A. TANEY, *Art Director*
JOSEPHINE B. BOLT, *Associate Art Director*
URSULA PERRIN, *Design Assistant*
RICHARD SCHLECHT, *Maps*
JOHN D. GARST, JR., MARGARET DEANE, MONICA
    W. LeBEAU, MILDA STONE, *Map Research*
    and Production

Production and Printing

ROBERT W. MESSER, *Production Manager*
MARGARET MURIN SKEKEL, RAJA D. MURSHED,
    Production Assistants
JOHN R. METCALFE, *Engraving and Printing*
JANE H. BUXTON, MARTA ISABEL COONS, SUZANNE
    J. JACOBSON, ELIZABETH VAN BEUREN JOY,
    PENELOPE A. LOEFFLER, JOAN PERRY,
    Staff Assistants
DOROTHY M. CORSON, BARBARA L. KLEIN, *Index*

Library of Congress CIP Data: page 199

*Slender mountain stream divides to encircle
the barn on a tiny farm rimmed by the autumn
forest near Great Smoky Mountains National
Park. Overleaf: Homeward bound, a young
squirrel hunter follows his dogs along
a shaded dirt road in northern Arkansas.
Page 1: Deft hands of an Ozark wood-carver
fashion a quail from a piece of linden wood.*

ENDPAPERS: GEORGE FOUNDS
HARD-COVER DESIGN: ARLINKA BLAIR

Foreword

DEEP IN THE HOLLOWS of my native West Virginia, on steep slopes, and along narrow river valleys, there still live a few hardy individuals who have spent their lives virtually in sight of their homes. Most of them—like their fellow mountaineers elsewhere—have a special bond with their hills. In spite of hardships they have chosen to remain there. Some might say "the mountains have a holt" on them. Others might call it "bein' part of the land."

Even as a youngster growing up in the state's southern coal fields, I sensed the magnetism of the mountains for the people who live among them. Years later, after my wife and I had left the Kanawha Valley to attend college in the Midwest, this affinity became still more apparent to me when my parents once visited us. They would like to leave West Virginia, they said, and come to live nearby. My father, a coal mine electrician for most of his life, quickly found work. But as we began to talk of moving vans and a new house, I noticed that he spoke with less and less enthusiasm. Finally he called me aside and said quietly, "I've decided not to make the change." And then he added, "You might not understand, but I would miss my mountains too much."

I did indeed understand.

Perhaps the attraction of the mountains stems from the feeling of strength they impart, offering security to those who share the valleys, coves, and slopes. Or it may come from a desire of the people to hold on to a simple, unhurried life—to dwell in the privacy a ridge or a hollow can offer, something outsiders might look upon as isolation. Perhaps the spell the mountains cast derives in part from the serenity they evoke, a serenity often enhanced by small things known to every mountaineer: moonlit ridges set against a darkening winter sky; the lingering echo of a locomotive whistle and the rumble of a train breaking the stillness of a valley in the middle of the night.

Simply, sensitively, through glimpses into the lives of American mountain people from the Appalachians to the Cascades, the photographer and the authors of this book have captured something of the "hold" of the mountains, and have revealed the strong spirit of independence that seems instilled in the people who live there. Those West Virginians who guided their mountain homeland to statehood more than a century ago no doubt knew that magnetism and sense of freedom. They surely meant for the motto they selected for their state to apply to all hill people the country over: *Montani Semper Liberi*—"Mountaineers are always free."

ROBERT L. BREEDEN

"Beginning on a buckeye standing in the branch,
thence up said branch to an ash, thence up
said branch to a beech..." reads the boundary
description detailed in the 19th-century deed
to the Sam Hughes farm near Roan Mountain,
Tennessee. Bill Hughes (right), Sam's brother,
discusses the meandering course of the property line
with Charlie Odum, owner of the adjoining land.

Contents

1

"A belief in the peculiar virtue of mountains"

by Charlton Ogburn

ANYONE who has been much among mountains and the people living in them could hardly read this letter in *The Denver Post* of May 7, 1972, without smiling: ". . . both my granddads . . . lived to be 90. Great Uncle Bill lived to be 102, Uncle Tom 89, Uncle Oscar 92 and Uncle Rice is going strong at 96. I left the Ozarks at the age of 20 and probably won't live to be old, as I am only 74 and have slipped somewhat." It was signed, "Bill Potts."

I came upon the letter while touring some of the country's principal highland areas. I was seeking an answer to a particular question: Is there such a thing as an American "mountain breed"?

I thought there was. Mountains seem to possess strong, often demanding personalities of their own. It seemed reasonable to me to expect that people who took to a life amid mountains and came under their continuing influence should have some characteristics in common.

Reasonable, yes. But could you really relate the southern Appalachian or Ozark highlanders, who for generations might almost have been called subnations of the United States, to those assorted Americans who scattered themselves through the mountains of the West, stayed simply because they liked what they found, and would never think of themselves as a people apart?

At the time I came on Mr. Potts's letter, I was contrasting Ben Kettle, who owns a 6,000-acre ranch under the snowy crests of Colorado's Sangre de Cristo Mountains, with a sawmill worker I had met in the Cumberlands a few weeks before. The grizzled West Virginian, whose build recalled one of those high crag-anchored trees toughened and twisted by the wind, had been a coal miner, and visibly enjoyed reviewing for my edification how things were in the deep galleries. "In the end, the whole business comes down. You can hear the supports snapping with the sound of cannons, and the mountain shakes the houses all around as she settles." He had had only a few years of schooling, and perhaps lived high in a hollow in a forlorn dwelling without plumbing. The other man was the model of a strapping Westerner. He held a doctorate in veterinary medicine. His wife was a journalist. His splendid "seed stock" herd of Herefords must have been one of the most thoroughly and persistently examined anywhere; the life histories of the animals filled ledgers.

Were the two men alike in any way?

I remember that as the West Virginian spoke of old stumps of oak and chestnut six or seven feet through, stumps he had seen as a boy, the light in his eyes was like that in Ben Kettle's when the rancher pointed to a window of the pioneer cabin that forms the nucleus of his house. Ben recounted how his grandparents would sometimes look up of an evening and see a Ute Indian or two peering through that same glass: "They would ask the visitors in and would feed them."

The cabin had been built a hundred years before, and I wished my West Virginian could see the polished, 5-by-10-inch, hand-hewn red spruce timbers of its walls and their neat dovetailing at the corners. I feel sure that he would have deeply approved, and would have enjoyed a sense of personal vindication which neither he nor I could have fully explained.

And if those two men suddenly were dropped into a wilderness, they would set about saving themselves in natural accord with each other, I have no doubt, and with similar resourcefulness, efficiency, and calm.

What that letter in *The Denver Post* set me to thinking was that mountain dwellers, as I have known them, are notably alike in their belief in the peculiar virtue of mountains.

Yes, they will concede, the mountains make you earn any crop you coax out of the thin soil of their slopes — "and break your neck if you was to trip while hoeing and fetch up at the bottom!" Or lead

(Continued on page 16)

Appalachian couple of about 1910 sit on the porch of their eastern Kentucky farmhouse. In isolated mountain communities a tradition of self-sufficiency developed — reflected here in homespun clothes and the handmade cane, clay pipe, and furniture.

APPALACHIAN MUSEUM, BEREA COLLEGE, KENTUCKY

9

*T*hree generations assemble for a family
reunion in the Missouri Ozarks at the turn of the
century. Food prepared by many hands weights
the table before the large log house. Strong family
ties and scattered mountain settlements underscored
the importance of social gatherings—and still do:
People travel considerable distances not only
for weddings and funerals but also to celebrate
baptisms, housewarmings, and barn-raisings.

APPALACHIAN MUSEUM, BEREA COLLEGE, KENTUCKY; C. 1915 ABOVE, C. 1920 BELOW

In eastern Tennessee about 1930, "Uncle" George Lamon rides a ground sled pulled by a bull. Mountaineers still use sleds to haul provisions over rough slopes, mud, or snow. Opposite, above, an Appalachian mother grinds grain by rotating the upper stone of a quern—two millstones set in a hollowed stump; the chute funnels the meal into a trough. A cast-iron stove heats the one-room cabin of a Kentucky lumberman; a sunbeam finds its way into the smoke-grimed fireplace, abandoned after the chimney crumbled.

𝒩eighbors join Peter Price (on the porch with a meal sack) at his gristmill on Tory Creek, Missouri, in 1905. A tailcoat distinguishes country doctor John M. Gideon. The abundant streams of the Ozarks once powered some 400 mills, and most became popular meeting places and social centers.

you on year after year with the promise of rich strikes or lost mines, and leave you only older and poorer. Or, piling the snow around you, drive you crazy with cabin fever, starve you, freeze you.

Still, the virtue of mountains wins out. If you are not done in along the way, they promote a long life. Bill Potts ascribed the longevity of his family to the Ozarks in general and to the local headcheese in particular. I have heard the salubrity of mountains attributed to the purity of their air and waters, and—in contradictory ways—to the altitude: The lower atmospheric pressure is either easier on the system (less oppressive), or else harder (putting greater demands on the heart and lungs) and thus fortifying. The sun comes stronger through the thinner air. And then there are the herbs.

Or it is simply that you live long in the mountains because they do not yield their bounty, such as it is, to halfhearted labor: They make you work. "When you're my age, it's being active that keeps you alive," a hog-breeder in southern Missouri said to me on my way to Forsyth. I had stopped to admire his shoats—150 of them—and he took me around the pens where big red sows were lying in inert expectancy or being nuzzled by black-and-white piglets. Like many Ozarkians, he had gone out into the world but in due course had returned to the country, having found nothing else he liked as well. "There were some retired from the railroad same time as I did who said all they were going to do from then on was sit. In a few months they were in the hospital, and pretty soon all were dead. That was 17 years ago."

Below the hog farm, in an idyllic setting of grass and trees, stood a small log cabin "built before you or me was born," said the breeder's hired man, a gaunt Ozarkian with that mountain way of addressing a stranger that seems half puzzled, half surprised. "About 85 or 90 years ago," said his employer. For a log cabin it was thus not terribly old, but all the same it recalled the frontier; when it was built there was still land for homesteading in the Ozarks. By its door a stream flowed musically over shelves of limestone. The road dipped into the water and thus qualified as a mountain road; none does, to me, unless it fords a stream. Beyond in the fresh, green May foliage, among flowers new to me, a blue grosbeak the color of lapis lazuli took wing, and a diminutive white-eyed vireo sang *Chick! O beware the wee bird! Chick!*

The stream met the river where it glided beneath a somber cliff of weathered limestone, laid down when fishes were first appearing, more than 400 million years ago. It struck me that the news here was not of the clash of armies across the world, but of a contest between two woodpeckers for a nesting cavity in a dead oak. One was a golden-shafted flicker, the other a stunningly handsome bird of blue-black and white with a ruby velvet head. I watched them until the flicker abandoned the cavity to (I suspected) its rightful owner. I had lost any sense of hurry. The fact recalled a memory from my boyhood when I was visiting Highlands, North Carolina. A woman was explaining the deliberate mountaineer manner. Nodding toward Rabun Bald and the Nantahalas, she said, "Those giants have been here for millions of years. What happens this minute or this day isn't going to decide the fate of the world." Perhaps that realization, too, is one of the things that set mountain dwellers apart.

The ultimate claim for the special virtue of mountains was made recently by William Thurgood, who runs a remarkably successful alcoholic rehabilitation center on a farm ringed by the Blue Ridge near Charlottesville, Virginia. "A man can't stand there and look at those mountains around and not know there is a higher power," he said.

From Mount McKinley (Denali, the Tall One, home of the sun to the Alaskan Indians) to Olympus (the citadel of Zeus) to Everest (Chomolungma, the Sherpas' goddess mother of the world), human beings have associated gods with mountains. They have done so since long before the psalmist declared, "I will lift up mine eyes unto the hills, from whence cometh my help." One is far less likely in the mountains than in a city of the plains, where the greatest structures are human, to imagine man to be supreme in the universe. An abiding respect for what lies beyond man's province, taking the form of a strong religious cast of mind, or fatalism, or a deep attentiveness to nature, or even a combination of all three: That may well be a mark of the confirmed mountaineer the world over.

Understandably enough, men have also looked to the mountains for refuge —including many who would not ordinarily have chosen to live there. The high country of the American West, as every watcher of screen or tube is aware, was made to order for desperadoes with booty across their saddle horns and posses at their heels. In the Great Smoky Mountains, hundreds of Cherokees found concealment in the 1830's when their fellows were being expelled to Oklahoma over the Trail of Tears; many of their descendants still live in the Smokies. On the far side of the Wasatch Range in Utah, the Mormons found asylum after they had been driven from Illinois in 1846.

Indeed, our most distinctive and far most numerous mountain people, occupying those parts of seven states that make up what we call southern Appalachia, came to escape societies organized to their disadvantage. Through much of the 18th century, land-hungry Protestants from northern Ireland poured into the American Colonies. They crossed the Atlantic to escape religious and economic discrimination such as had driven their English and lowland Scottish forebears to cross the Irish Sea a century before. In quest of land, many who arrived in Philadelphia—as well as some Pennsylvania *Deutsch* who had decided to move on—pressed down the Great Valley of

*O*zark girls pose in a dray for an itinerant photographer about 1900. The flowers and white dresses suggest Easter or Graduation Day; or the photographer's infrequent visit may have provided reason enough to dress up and to harness the horse. The well-built house— clapboards, cornices, brick chimney— belonged to a prosperous family.

the Appalachians into Virginia, North Carolina, and Tennessee. There they were joined by families from the southern colonies who had started migrating westward. Scotch-Irish, English, and some Welsh and Germans: These were the settlers of the southern Appalachians.

It was largely their offspring who settled the Ozarks, as successive generations of big families populated the eastern mountains. Within 20 years after the Louisiana Purchase, many were crossing the Mississippi — along with adventurous loners heading for the beaver streams of the distant Rockies — to find new homes in Missouri and Arkansas.

Why didn't they occupy the rich lowlands of the new region? I asked that of one of their descendants, James Morris, who achieved national fame with radio's Grand Ole Opry as Jimmy Driftwood. I had found him riding a tractor on his farm in Timbo, Arkansas.

"They did — and they came down with what they called chills: malaria. After that, the cool, dry Ozark high country looked mighty good. Besides, it reminded them of home. They flocked to it. And they sent word back to relatives." Like all good hillsmen, Jimmy has a lively sense of the past, for the hills speak powerfully of continuity. He recalls nostalgically and vividly the events of his boyhood, including a three-weeks-long trip to Oklahoma with his parents in the days of primitive roads and open range.

But such journeys were not common. Through the 19th century and the first third of the 20th, most southern highlanders on both sides of the Mississippi lived relatively isolated from the rest of the world. The Appalachian ranges have been carved deeply and intricately by twisting streams carrying the heavy rains of millions of years. Communication beyond the steep ridges was difficult. The invaders of this land were thrown on their own devices and the resources of the hills for most of their requirements. Preserving the Elizabethan idiom they had brought with them, and for their solace the ballads of an even earlier time, they developed the crafts that have come to be held in such high regard in modern-day, mass-production America.

If you come to the Ozarks from the north, you do not see at first why they should have imposed any isolation on the settlers. The horizon is nearly level. The feeling grows that you are in mountainous country without mountains, albeit much cut by valleys. Understanding of the terrain grows as you travel. The Ozark highlands take in an enormous area of southern Missouri, northern Arkansas, and eastern Oklahoma. The farther south you go through the Ozarks and into the Ouachitas, the more respectable in size the hills become. But it was the distances as much as the obstacles facing road builders that tended to keep the highlanders to themselves. Even today you can drive mile upon mile in the back country and see little but woods near and far, interspersed with pastureland for beef cattle.

Crop farming is nearly gone. "The roads have put an end to it," said J. R. McNeill, an Ozark youth who was chiseling a two-foot-high figure of a mountaineer from a sassafras log in Peter Engler's wood-carving shop at Reeds Spring, Missouri. "You can make a lot more on construction jobs, if you can drive to them, than by raising crops." Nevertheless the drivers cling to their homesteads, tucked away in the valleys. "You couldn't root them out!" exclaimed a red-haired young woman in an antique shop in Omaha, Arkansas, when I asked if there were really Ozarkians back in those wooded hills. "Only they've been changed by shoes and television," added a stocky, graying helper with half-quizzical humor, apparently a countryman himself.

Yes, television has come to the highlands, but not with complete reliability. Bill Weatherly, representing the fourth generation to farm beside Weatherly Creek in the Umpqua Valley of Oregon, told me that the lead-in wire from his antenna up the hill had been hooked and carried off shortly before by some elk.

There are still cabins in the hollows and on the ridges of the southern Appalachians accessible only by four-wheel-drive — some, in fact, only by horse or on foot. As recently as 1959, newspaperman

Hank Burchard, putting himself to the test of living off the country in a wild part of his ancestral North Carolina mountains, came on a small, inbred community miles from a road and so out of touch that its members fled at his approach and could only gradually be coaxed back. But physical and cultural isolation is largely a thing of the past in Appalachia, and entirely so in the Ozarks.

Yet ingrained habits of mind and turns of temperament are not quickly lost. Even today among the southern highlanders can be recognized the pride, independence of spirit, toughness of fiber, and attachment to place without which these people could not have endured the privations and hardships that were their lot for two centuries. And I believe such traits are generally typical of men and women who make their home in the mountains, both those who were born there and those who have chosen to come and stay. Physical isolation in the western mountains, where there has never been any real cultural apartness, can be acute. It is no less so for being chiefly seasonal—a matter of being snowbound, or of herding sheep in the summer on high grazing lands where no other human being may appear for weeks on end.

Mountain people share a need to be well away from the press of humanity, to keep a buffer of woods or chaparral between them and the throng, to enjoy a sense of space around them. To thrive on separation requires a spiritual self-reliance and hardihood and even, perhaps, a certain solitariness of soul. With this, I believe, goes a bent for craftsmanship, a capacity to be content and absorbed in the practice of the woodsman's arts, the working of clay on a wheel, the pressing of knife or chisel to a smooth, yielding

𝒲eary miners and a woman visitor—a rarity in the gold fields—pause beside a "long tom," or placer-mining trough, in a ravine near Auburn, California, in 1852. Spurred by the 1848 discovery of gold at Sutter's Mill, thousands of Easterners swarmed to tent camps in the foothills of the Sierra Nevada. For the great majority, the dream of hitting pay dirt quickly and then returning home to a life of luxury soon gave way to the realities of hardship and disease.

grain, the weaving of white-oak splits in basketry, or perhaps the tooling of leather. A contemplative resident of Nevada City in the Sierra Nevada whom Bruce Dale met while taking photographs for this book offered the view that the beauty of their surroundings influences the mountain people as craftsmen; he may well be right.

None of this is to argue that mountain dwellers are misanthropic. Quite the contrary. The shyness of an inherent solitariness; anticipation of condescension on the part of a more affluent stranger; wariness of the outside world, often justified by bitter experience: These qualities have given mountain people a reputation for being standoffish. But those who know them agree that they are characteristically warm, hospitable, and outgoing once their apprehensions are set at rest. With a good listener, they tend to be great talkers—great reminiscers. And the swapping of tall tales is still a favorite mountain pastime.

Among southern highlanders, even those whose cabins were perched on hogbacks farthest from the road's end, the bonds of community have generally been strong and those of family stronger still. Clan solidarity, and the tendency of feelings to be intense when concentrated on relatively few other people, gave rise to the notorious mountain feuds. These were most devastating in the Cumberlands, where the population is split among narrow valleys walled in by steep hills. There the French-Eversole, Hatfield-McCoy, and "Bloody Breathitt" feuds were murderous affairs, as were the "Bald Knobbers" episodes in the Ozarks. But it was not because the participants were what we would normally consider murderers, not that they were antisocial, but rather that human bonds counted so much with them—and that they were fiercely independent, impulsive, and fearless. In uniform, fighting in a cause they believed in, such men have made superior soldiers from King's Mountain to the Argonne and Saipan.

Glen Young was not at home when Steve Wennstrom took me to meet him,

(Continued on page 24)

Sense of humor helps a Rocky Mountain prospector stick it out during the gold-strike days of the 1860's in Colorado and Utah. Seeking escape from prolonged economic depression, adventurers with nothing "but a blanket and a brazen face"— many of whom had earlier tried their luck in California—took up the cry of "Pike's Peak or Bust!" Entrepreneurs prospered: A barber could set up shop with an empty barrel, wood blocks for foot rests, and some courtesy whiskey for the customers.

Water jet wears away a Colorado slope in a
late 19th-century example of hydraulic mining.
Western mining rapidly evolved from panning by
individuals into large-scale and often destructive
operations by companies employing hundreds.
Lumbermen, looking upon the vast forests of great
trees as an inexhaustible supply, began to strip
the mountains of California. At right, workers rest
on a coast redwood trunk about ten feet in diameter.

but his home in Oregon's Siskiyou Mountains was in itself worth a trip to see. There were cabins he had built here and there, odd pieces of machinery and hoses running this way and that, all probably related to the one-man gold-mining operation he had afoot. There was no electricity, but a washing machine was hooked up to what appeared to be a small water turbine. It was a modern, Western version of the pioneer Appalachian mountaineer's farm. The farther back into the mountains you go, the more self-contained are the homesteads you find, and the more the versatility of the homesteaders is in evidence. That is one reason you feel, going deep into the mountains, that you are returning to the past.

And it is true that the nearest you can come now to the frontier of old is where the land stands steep and lofty. In the highlands of both East and West, men look out on a still-wild America of deep forests or high heath roamed by deer, bears, and wildcats, or pumas and bighorns, and patrolled by soaring ravens and eagles. Bold summits rear majestically against the sky, reminding men of the provisional nature of their triumphs. There is a spirit of wilderness that cannot be mistaken where it still breathes. More tenacious than might be supposed, it is still a presence in the lives of the mountain dwellers, as it was for the earliest Americans.

Finally, there is the realization that the mountain people are where they are for reasons akin to those that brought settlers to the New World to begin with. Succinctly expressed, it is from a desire to be out from under. Perhaps the mountain people all tend to be in some degree what the southern highlanders are often called: our living ancestors.

To be out from under comes easily if you have money, but only with sacrifices if you have not. And often one of the sacrifices is giving up the opportunity to make much money; that is a price most mountain people pay for what means more to them.

Ironically enough, much of the earth's wealth is stored in the mountains. It is there that nature makes accessible metallic ores, coal, construction stone. In the mountains the timber still grows when the lowlands have been stripped. The highlands harbor furbearers. But the day of striking it rich as an individual —if it ever existed for more than a handful—is gone. The small placer miner, the mill operator, the trapper have long since acknowledged that the wealth of the mountains yields principally to generously capitalized corporations.

The big mining and lumbering companies do provide jobs—hundreds of thousands of them—and the automobile enables their employees to live at home in the hills and get back and forth to work. I met one who combined two lives very successfully up in the Coast Range above Drain, Oregon. Said a sign on a gate: *Bar W Ranch. Romneys. Suffolks.* When I had driven higher and looked back, I saw as picturesque a sheep ranch as could be imagined, a few small buildings clustered on a green carpet saddled on a mountain shoulder. Unable to resist returning, I was met by a genial woman, Helen Woolley—surely a grand name for sheep ranchers—who said her husband, John, was off "falling in the woods." Smiling at my blank expression, she explained that this meant cutting trees down; he was with a logging company. He soon appeared, his outdoorsman's complexion set off by blue eyes. He put in a full work-week with the chain saw; it paid the bills. But, showing me the clever hay-feeders he had built in the large shed in which the sheep sheltered, he declared his intention to prove in time that the farm of itself could support a family.

Unfortunately the wealth produced in the mountains has by no means brought about commensurate economic opportunity for the mountain people. Poverty in Appalachia is notorious. For all the hundreds of millions of dollars in coal and lumber that have been taken out of the Cumberlands, the region's per capita income today is among the lowest in the nation.

The miners are far better paid than in the past, but many are not employed full time, and mining remains a dangerous occupation. The deaths of 91 underground workers in an Idaho silver mine in 1972 reminded us that the hazards are not confined to the coal fields.

While machines have relieved the miner and the logger of much backbreaking toil, they also have reduced the number of men needed for a given output. Considerably more coal is being produced in Appalachia today than half a century ago —with about a third as many miners.

The more powerful the machines, the more damage they can inflict. In the Sierra 120 years ago, mine owners introduced hydraulic mining systems with pumps capable of directing at a mountainside a jet of water strong enough to kill a man at 200 feet. It was an effective method of washing gold out of hiding—and it buried the valleys below in rubble. Today, strip-mining bulldozers and power shovels have gouged 20,000 miles of step out of the flanks of the Appalachians to expose the coal.

As for logging, one of the arguments for clear-cutting heard in the West is that in selective cutting, the machines do such injury to trees left standing that a clean sweep might as well be made. Telling me of the trail a log-skidder leaves dragging a tree down a mountainside, the Cumberlands sawmill worker said wryly, "Ain't nobody cares much for poor old West Virginia." His remark came back to me when I was comparing him with Ben Kettle, and thought of how the rancher had spoken of developers' seeking to subdivide a tract for summer homes next to the national forest above his place: "All it would take to start gullying is some trail cycles wearing paths."

Stock certificate issued in 1893 conveys 500 shares of a Colorado mining venture. Many Easterners did their prospecting from a distance by investing in corporations that ranged from legitimate operators to fraudulent firms able to produce certificates in abundance, but no ore.

(Continued on page 30)

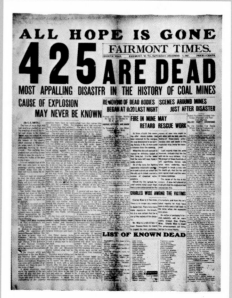

Massed coffins at Monongah, West Virginia, contain the bodies of coal workers killed when two mines exploded on December 6, 1907. Headlines proclaimed what still ranks as the worst mining disaster in the nation's history; the actual toll: 361. Growing outrage over mining conditions focused attention on generally lax safety standards. Critics also publicized the use of draft animals (opposite), consigned underground for life.

$\mathcal{E}$victed from company-owned houses, striking miners and their
families await transportation from Pursglove, West Virginia, in
October 1924. Demanding recognition and reform, the United Mine
Workers organized strikes against mine operators in the coal fields
of Appalachia and Colorado beginning in 1912. The companies,
employing strikebreakers and detectives and often backed by state
militia, granted few concessions to the miners. Violence flared
on both sides; when in 1914 dynamiters blew up and burned a tent
colony of miners' families at Ludlow, Colorado, 20 people died,
11 of them children. Opposite, militia volunteers under Lt. Karl
(Butch) Linderfelt, at far right, ride to disperse the tent occupants.

I asked Ben and his wife if the panorama of snow-crusted peaks rising before them—one of the most stunning I have ever seen—still meant something to them after all these years. They fairly exploded with enthusiasm. "It's always different, hour by hour, every day, and it's always beautiful," declared Elizabeth Kettle. "Most impressive of all, once in a while just before sunrise, mysteriously, the whole range will glow red!" Thus Sangre de Cristo: blood of Christ.

From other mountain dwellers I have heard similar affirmations. Said Helen Woolley, "Oh, no, you never get so you take the beauty of the mountains for granted." When finally the Woolleys turn over the Bar W to their children, they intend to move—higher up the mountain! At a restaurant in Branson, Missouri, when I asked my waitress why she and her husband had moved back from St. Joseph, she exclaimed, "Why, he just likes the hills! If he walks one mile on a weekend, he must walk 20."

Bill Weatherly of Weatherly Creek was born in Portland, but as a boy he used to visit the farm his great-grandfather had bought in 1880, and he hiked and hunted the surrounding mountains; and finally as a man he had to come back to live. He raises sheep and Hereford cattle, and grows barley and oats on his 350 acres, but he told me that he cannot make farming pay. If his son can keep the farm, it will be because his living comes from forestry. "I'm going broke," Bill said; then, his aquiline face lighted by one of his ready smiles, he added, "and enjoying every minute of it."

There has long been an exodus from Appalachia; the region cannot support its offspring. But those who leave do not forget. The annual family reunions are witness to that. Hank Burchard tells me that when his mother's people get together near Bryson City, on the edge of the Smokies, as many as a thousand gather for the feast laid out on a hundred-foot-long table of wire hardware cloth stretched on sawhorses.

Home has a hold on us nothing ever entirely dislodges. When home is in the mountains, the hold seems to be especially strong. To understand their power you have to go among them yourself. You find, as I found, the truth of what a Georgia friend said about evening in the mountains, when dusk collects like a shadowy sea in the cove: The earth is possessed by peace.

I remember such a time in my seventh year, when I was visiting a great aunt near Franklin, North Carolina; and ever since I have associated the spell with the distant sound of cowbells I heard then. It came back to me not long ago in the Ozarks when a bell sounded from down in a hollow. I was walking along a high road, looking far out across green fields and reaches of woodland. And I was thinking how, in the city, you forget in time what silence is. You are unprepared to have it so quiet, with no sound at all but the whisper of the wind and the keening of a meadowlark. It comes to you that when the human din is stilled, and only then, the universal voice has a chance to be heard.

In the Colorado Rockies, while I was walking up a gulch near Central City, it was the distant wail of a locomotive that emphasized the silence. In the mountains, I thought, there is a feeling of recovering a lost America. Here I could get back to the essential dignity of the earth. It was in the ancient, solid granite and gneiss of the high canyon walls, and in the tumbling, warbling stream. It was in the great, humped, snow-frosted mountains, bristling with forests of spruce, and in the thin, chill wind that seemed to come straight from the pure, undefiled source of all winds.

Winter still lingered above 8,000 feet in the Rockies; and in central Oregon a few days later, on May 10, the Three Sisters at the head of the McKenzie Valley appeared to be covered by glistening marshmallow sauce. But lower down, along a steep logging road I was hiking, wild flowers were blooming in colorful variety. I heard only a faint rushing sound; it could have been the voice of falling waters, from which the Cascades take their name, or perhaps it was the wind in the tops of the tall, straight Douglas firs. Engulfed by the quiet, I felt possessed by the mountain I was climbing, and by its neighbors, on which the spired trees crowded to the summits. The loneliness was almost tangible. But with the loneliness comes something of great importance to the committed mountain dweller: In a way not easy to define but nonetheless real, the lonely heights and the green vales far from the crowded, jostling lowlands mean safety.

If mountain people do not command many resources, there is one at hand for which demand down in those same crowded, jostling lowlands is great and growing. That is the special appeal of the mountains as a temporary retreat—the appeal of grandeur and solitude—to present and potential visitors. The mountains are steadily growing in popularity with vacationists, summer and winter. The visitors will diminish the seclusion that is one of the mountains' chief attractions; on the other hand, they may well constitute a potent force for the protection of the mountains against the abuses that despoil them, and for the repair, as far as possible, of the damage that has been done. They also will mean income for mountain people who otherwise might not survive. And surely many will come not just for recreation but for what they can learn.

Our "living ancestors" have formed reservoirs of much that the rest of us have been in peril of losing. On my first visit to the town of Highlands in 1928, I had to have explained to me a kind of dancing practiced there. It was called square dancing. In recent years the ballads of the mountains have enormously influenced the nation's musical tastes. Organizations like the Southern Highland Handicraft Guild, by helping to market handiwork products, have contributed to a renaissance of crafts in the mountains and elsewhere. And along with our coming to appreciate such articles, many of us have also learned that turning raw materials into finished objects of beauty with our own hands can give a vital sense of fulfillment in a specialized, technological society.

Mountain folk provide not only prac-titioners and teachers but natural pupils. In a valley of the Klamath Mountains, a friend and I gave a ride to a young woman who had recently moved from the city with her husband and some others similarly inspired; she was on her way to the schoolhouse where she and some friends were teaching the children various kinds of needlework.

From 1934 until quite recently, Mary Hambidge of Rabun Gap, Georgia, engaged men and women of the mountain farms in the raising and shearing of sheep, the carding and dyeing of wool, and the weaving of textiles that sold in fashionable New York shops. "The most remarkable woman I have ever met," Eliot Wigginton calls her.

Mr. Wigginton is the teacher who set his English class at Rabun Gap - Nacoochee School to interviewing the students' grandparents and other old-timers on the traditional wisdom and skills of the mountains, from planting by the signs of the zodiac to churning butter—"affairs of plain living"—and publishing the lore thus gleaned in the magazine *Foxfire*. Selections from it have been republished in *The Foxfire Book*, to immediate acclaim and amazing sales success.

"Appalachia has what America must regain—a closeness with the earth," says a contributor to the magazine *Mountain Life and Work*. James Morris—Jimmy Driftwood—would agree. At his farm he puts up 200 people at a time who come to attend the Mountain View, Arkansas, folk music festivals for which he is responsible. He conducted me proudly around the new festival auditorium being constructed of dark native sandstone, along with harmonizing buildings in which a score of crafts will be demonstrated and the products sold.

"Last weekend, the three-day festival attracted more than 80,000 visitors," he said. Why do so many come? "They're looking for reality. They're trying to find their roots."

For that, they could surely do worse than to seek among the mountain people, who know that there are priceless satisfactions that elude us in the struggle for power and material advantage.

2

Southern Appalachia: "We call ourselves hillbillies"

by Bill Peterson

I DON'T EVER EXPECT James Maggard to call me a friend. I'm too young, too citified, not enough of a woodsman. "The old-time people are what suits me best," he told me one morning as we sat on his front porch, listening to the worn boards creak beneath our rockers and a gentle breeze ripple the poplar and wild cherry trees. He spoke with no trace of discourtesy, and I understood. "It always seems good to get with anyone I'm used to," he said.

James, rail-thin and spry at 81, is one of the last of the old hillbillies, a direct descendant of the independent, free spirits who tamed the wilderness 200 years ago. He, his wife, and one son live in a small, weather-bleached cabin that until a few years ago had a dirt floor. It sits near the summit of Pine Mountain, a peak that rises a thousand feet above the Cumberland Plateau in Letcher County, Kentucky. He was born nearby in Virginia, and his father spent most of his life on the mountain, living by scratch farming, hunting wild game, and moonshining.

It was the rugged, sometimes bitterly cruel life of the woodsman-pioneer that he passed on to his children, one where a man had to struggle merely to survive. But it is the only life James has ever known, and even today he seldom leaves the mountain. When he does, perhaps once a month, it is to buy supplies at Bowman's Grocery on the Poor Fork of the Cumberland River, or to visit an eye doctor in Whitesburg, the county seat. James doesn't like Whitesburg, a metropolis of 1,100 souls, or any other city he's ever been in.

It was a bright afternoon in early June when I first visited the Maggard place, at the end of a bumpy gravel track passable only by foot, horse, or jeep.

James wasn't home. "He's huntin' somewhere up that mountain," his son Claude told me as we sat down in the shade of the hog shed, a structure made of logs. "He can't stay in a house hardly at all." James's eyes have gone bad, and he probably couldn't hit a gray squirrel if it crossed his path. Nevertheless he takes his .22-caliber rifle from its perch on the bedroom wall every day, in season and out, and wanders toward the summit of Pine Mountain.

After a while two small yellow dogs crashed through the underbrush. James followed, wearing an old straw hat and a worn black suit coat over his denim overalls. He greeted us warmly, then squatted beside the hog shed, his rifle resting across his knees.

I asked about his reputation as a sharpshooter, and his clear blue eyes lit up.

"Boy, I could shoot, I could shoot," he said. "Lord, the satisfaction them old hog rifles could give a man. I'd rather shoot than eat in the old days. Why, I've shot as many as 15 squirrels and never missed a one."

Wild turkeys once roamed the mountain, he said slowly. The biggest one he ever shot was "way back in Bad Branch." He hit it twice, but it refused to die.

"For the longest time I couldn't find 'im nowhere," he continued, his voice picking up speed. "Then comes this shower of rain and I heard 'im breakin' branches like a horse. I throwed that gun against the ground and away I went. I jumped on that big gobbler and got him by the neck. I said, 'Old buddy, if you go this time I'll be damned if you won't have to take me with you.' I held that old gentleman right by his neck till I knew his last breath was gone."

In many of his stories, James is first the victim, then the hero. Folklorists call the type "Jack tales," and say it goes back for centuries. In such yarns the hero, like Jack in "Jack and the Beanstalk," becomes the innocent pawn of circumstance and plunges into one predicament after another until he finally prevails because of his native cunning.

James's stories dwell on the past, the good old days when the pioneer spirit wasn't just something to read about in history books. His friends from those years have either died or adapted to changing times. James's life, however, has changed remarkably little. He still picks wild fruit and berries; grows a huge garden; keeps bees, hogs, and a cow; sells ginseng, a wild root that pharmaceutical

(Continued on page 40)

Veterans of the austere life of southern Appalachia, James Maggard, 81, and his wife, Diana, exemplify the tough-fibered mountaineers who have passed on the spirit, skills, and traditions of the early settlers.

Forested ridges of Harlan County, Kentucky, rise above an ocean of early-morning fog.

The nearby Cumberland Gap has funneled pioneers and travelers westward for 200 years.

Golden (Bunt) Howard, 46, who farms two acres near Hyden, Kentucky, plows a hillside cornfield only half a mile from his birthplace. Bunt dislikes cities: "It bothers me to sit in a town," he says. On a Kentucky porch, beans dry on strings suspended beside potted plants. Near Washington, Virginia, the yearly ritual of hog butchering includes scalding and scraping to remove bristles. Dressed and cured, the hogs provide pork products for months.

Warm glow of a lighted window welcomes home a Kentucky
mountaineer at day's end. Hollows throughout the
southern Appalachians shelter similar small homesteads.
A garden, some chickens, a milk cow, and sometimes a few
hogs make many of them almost self-sufficient when cash
runs short. Many a mountain family has set deep roots
in such a spot, never tiring of the pageant of changing
seasons that unfolds on the familiar wooded hillsides.

firms use in medicines; and lives in a four-room clapboard house uncomplicated by such modern conveniences as indoor plumbing.

Until recent years, when he was told his activities would jeopardize his old-age assistance check and perhaps land him a permanent prison cell, James was also a moonshiner. His white lightning sold for as much as $20 a gallon, and sometimes he'd carry glass jars of it 30 miles over the rugged mountains to a customer. Brushes with the law came frequently.

On one occasion, revenue agents caught him redhanded at a still. "Mercy, we had some of the finest whiskey ever made," James recalled. "Oh, did I hate to see it go to waste!" He pleaded with the agents for just one sip, and they finally agreed.

A sly grin crept across his creviced face as he continued the tale. "I took that old jug and I threw back my head as far as I could. I just let that whiskey flow fast as water. One of them revenuers yelled, 'That old man is going to be so drunk we'll have to carry him up the hill.' Sure enough, they had to. Lord o' mercy, I couldn't see to walk."

On a few remote hillsides the spirit of the past and the traditions of the moonshiner survive. It is a proud heritage that dates back to the days before the Revolutionary War when Scotch-Irish immigrants settled in the foothills of the Appalachians, bringing with them a knowledge of whiskey making and a hatred of British excise taxes.

But today's moonshiner is driven by competition to produce an ever-cheaper liquor, and the quality of his product has suffered; in some cases it is actually poisonous, because some condensers are made from old automobile radiators whose soldered joints can contaminate the product with lead salts.

Practicing moonshiners are understandably leery of strangers. I spent many days in the back country of Kentucky and Georgia searching for a still operator to talk to. Finally, in late November, I found myself on a narrow ribbon of dirt road winding up a wooded hillside. My guide informed me that law officers had never caught the moonshiner we were about to visit.

After several wrenching miles, I saw a sagging, unpainted cabin on stilts at the foot of a steep hill. A wisp of coal smoke rose above it. The yard was strewn with tin cans and rusty farm tools. A dog huddled under the porch, away from the chill rain, and three chickens pecked at the mud; but the moonshiner wasn't home. Several hours later we found him at his father's place two miles away, sipping a can of factory-made beer.

He was a husky man of about 35. He hadn't made a moonshine "run" for two months, he said—not since a utility crew uncovered his still while clearing brush for a new line—but with the holidays approaching, he was planning to emerge from retirement.

He had inherited his craft from his father, a lean, white-haired man of 68 who made his first illegal whiskey when he was only 8 years old—when it was, he explained, a question of economic necessity. Moonshining was one of the few ways a mountaineer could earn cash in the early 1900's; its profits fed and clothed many a family. "Everyone did it in this country in those days," he said.

Both father and son pride themselves on never having spent a night in jail for their moonshine activities. The closest either came was during Prohibition.

"Them days you could draw a big witness claim—sometimes as much as $30—from the Government for goin' down and tellin' about your neighbor makin' whiskey," the older man said. "Those were hard times and people needed the money. It got so dangerous you hardly dared to make any moonshine. If you ever got a drink you'd go wild."

Despite the danger, the old man made a moonshine run just before Christmas one year, and sold most of it to an untrustworthy cousin. Several days later, his wife glanced out a window and saw federal revenue agents climbing the path. "I ran out back and covered the still with brush. It was snowin' right smart. Hard to see. My wife poured the moonshine we had left into teakettles on the stove. Them revenuers hunted all over the place, but they never found it."

His son has tried farming and lumbering, and worked on a federal job-training program, but prefers hunting and moonshining to more conventional occupations; often he relies on Government food stamps to buy groceries for his family. He hides his crude still, fashioned from old barrels and copper sheeting, in a thicket 50 yards from his house. A creek provides an ample supply of clear water. "The law's never bothered me," he said, almost boastfully. "Selling it to the wrong people is what usually gets you. I know plenty of folks I'd never sell to."

In any event not everyone is a potential customer. The taste for moonshine is an acquired one—the flavor is somewhat akin to that of rubbing alcohol—and many mountaineers find they prefer store-bought bourbon, "red whiskey." The young moonshiner has two "safe" markets: old friends, and a few trusted bootleggers in those eastern Kentucky counties that have chosen to remain dry. He sells his product for $10 a gallon jar—about half as much as his father got during Prohibition. The demand just isn't there anymore. Nor are the moonshiners. In fiscal 1972, Government agents found only 2,981 stills to smash up, down from 14,000 as late as 1956. "Pretty soon there won't be none of us left," the son said. "Young folks just don't want to fool with it no more."

Parts of seven states share the southern Appalachians. Round-shouldered with age, the mountains thrust few peaks higher than 6,000 feet; nevertheless they have provided man with splendid scenery as well as timber and minerals.

Not only the moonshiners but also the woodsmen will soon be gone forever from the Appalachians. Already the strip miners' bulldozers and the loggers' chain saws have ravaged their beautiful hills and choked their once-clear streams with silt and acid. Already long-term dependence on public welfare has sapped the pride of many of their children. Already thousands of others have been driven from the land by the region's poverty.

Rich memories linger in those who remain. "We call ourselves hillbillies," they told me matter-of-factly; it's a name that carries no stigma, one that falls on anyone born in the hills. For generations, the mountains have hemmed them in. Some say they have become suspicious, standoffish. But I have found them kind and generous people, eager to share their front porches, fireplaces, and meals with a curious stranger—and eager to share the past.

Redwine Anderson was plowing in the April sun behind his two mules, Pearl and Jack. "Git-tee-up . . . git-tee-up, boy," he directed as the mules plodded slowly across his sandy bottomland beside the Middle Fork of the Kentucky River.

Redwine is sturdy and muscular at 68, his leathery face tanned by the mountain sun. He has used mules ever since he can remember.

"I don't work 'em too hard," he said, pausing at the edge of the field. "I figure a mule's like a person. You treat him right, he'll treat you right."

He has a special affection for this land. "I was raised mostly at that house over there," he said, pointing to a neat frame building a quarter mile away.

When Redwine was a boy, lumbermen cut the thick stands of oak, beech, and poplar from the steep hillsides around the farm. In the winter, they stacked the logs beside the river and lashed them together into rafts. When the spring floods came—"high tides," the mountain people call them—the men would jump atop the rafts and ride them to lumber mills as far away as Frankfort, Kentucky, a three-day trip by water. Sometimes Redwine would help—the only times he's ever done anything but farm.

Now, a half century later, another growth of timber graces the mountainsides. But Redwine and the other farmers of Breathitt County are acutely aware that all is not well. Vast hardships have fallen on the people of eastern Kentucky, driving 197,000 of them from their homes since 1950 and casting many of those who remain onto public welfare rolls.

Redwine doesn't believe in handouts. "My daddy brought me up to work," he said. "He was a working man. He learnt me how to work, and that's what I've always done."

Redwine stood in the hot sun, his thumbs hooked in the straps of his overalls. It's impossible to live in a place like Breathitt County, he said, where more than half of the residents depend on public assistance, and not be affected by the welfare culture.

"You can't hardly get no help no more. People who would've helped you are on this 'Happy Pappy' program [a U. S. Labor Department project for older workers]. Others are gettin' them food stamps. If they go in and explain they ain't makin' no money, they get 'em almost free. If they're workin', they got to pay for 'em. Don't give a man much reason to work."

A sudden wind kicked up a cloud of dust. Redwine watched it blow across the field, then picked up the plow reins and slapped Pearl, his favorite mule, across the flank. "Got to get goin'," he said. "Soon as a man stops workin', he starts dryin' up."

Arthur Dixon agreed. His home is in Whitesburg, Kentucky, but he hasn't let town living dispel his mountain ways or zeal for work. "I was born and raised in an old log house, daubed with mud, at the head of Elk Creek," he said. "Only one window in the whole place."

Judge Dixon is a craftsman, perhaps the last great Kentucky gunsmith. It's a skill he developed in retirement. He was 65 and had served 28 years in public office when his last term as Letcher County judge expired in 1962. "I realized I'd go crazy unless I had something to do," he said. "I'd made a few things— guns and dulcimers, mostly. So I got myself some books and went to work. Didn't realize what I was getting into."

(Continued on page 56)

Versatile farmer John Caldwell, 70, shapes a wagon brace from glowing metal. In his smithy in a shallow cave near his house, he produces rakes, hoes, knives, hinges, and plowshares.

Crossing a harvested field, John Caldwell
and his wife, Lottie, walk homeward
from the blacksmith shop. Between the
house and the road runs Laurel Fork;
a single log spans it as a footbridge.
John has been farming in these hills
for more than 50 years, raising
tobacco, corn, and vegetables. Lottie
gathers wild greens from slopes and creek
beds nearby. John, an avid coon hunter,
also likes to catch rattlesnakes, and
searches out bee trees: "Never was a man
loved to outwit wild things like me."
At left, the Caldwells' daughter Fannie
Mae strips tobacco after curing.

Arrival of the mail brings a young trio to a remote box
in Knott County, Kentucky. The mailman, Irvin Pratt, 70,
has ridden the 18-mile mountain route from Pine Top to
Pippa Passes off and on since 1955, and has worn out two
mules and three horses. He delivers "anything within reason,"
but has stopped toting such loads as mail-order tires.

Before an ancient potbellied stove, teacher Charles H. Osborne drills his charges
in the time-honored three R's at Sandy Fork School. Good-natured messages appear
in chalk (below) on an outside wall. The little school near Roark, Kentucky,
closed its doors for the last time in the summer of 1971 when authorities decided to
consolidate Sandy Fork with nearby Jack's Creek Settlement School. One-room school-
houses have nearly disappeared from the southern Appalachians. On a drowsy day at
Double Creek School near Hyden, a student (above) gazes pensively from a window.

Youngsters peer from the doorway of their
weathered stilt house near Mountain City, Georgia.
Although poverty and a plundered landscape
surround many Appalachian children, their
friendliness and plucky good humor strike nearly
all visitors. Pop-bottle scavengers (below)
patrol a roadside ditch near Manchester, Kentucky.
The boys sometimes earn $3 to $4 by gathering
and selling the bottles for a nickel apiece.

Charlottie Sparks and Harm
Holland, Tildy Peck's parents,
reared 14 children on Tar Ridge,
Kentucky, "and we never did go
hungry," says Tildy. Mrs.
Holland cooked in a fireplace,
and made soap for the neighborhood. As a young man, Harm
once walked to Arkansas and
back to visit his brothers —
almost a thousand miles.

Absorbed in her work, 86-year-old Matilda
(Tildy) Peck of Campton, Kentucky,
stitches a quilt in the soft daylight of
late afternoon. Tildy began quilting after
her six children and two stepchildren had
grown up. How many quilts has
she made? "Laws! I bet you couldn't stack
'em in this house." She used to organize
quilting bees, attracting a company of
neighbors. "We had fun," says Tildy. "I'd
kill a hen and make dumplings." Opposite,
bright patchwork butterflies flutter across
one of her favorite designs. A long lifetime of hard work has left her good-natured
and contented. "It's only just here
lately that I've taken to bein' ornery and
just sittin' around quiltin'," she says.

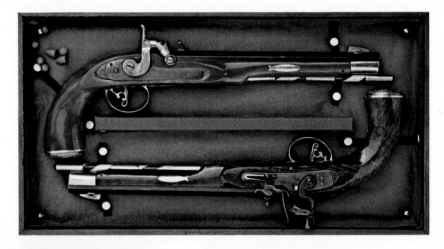

Carefully following a plan, Arthur Dixon shapes the curly-maple stock of a Kentucky long rifle. "I make every gun like it was the last one I'll ever get a chance at," says the retired judge. Upon leaving public service after 28 years, he realized he "had to have something to do," and took up the handcrafting of rifles, dulcimers, and pistols in his basement workshop in Whitesburg, Kentucky. He made the set of pistols above for his two grandsons. Judge Dixon has stopped accepting orders for his work: "I'm 75 years old, and I'll probably not be able to fill the orders I have on file now."

The results of his craftsmanship were scattered around his well-equipped basement workshop: Kentucky long rifles, their stocks fashioned from the finest curly maple, and authentic down to the silver patch box at the butt; curved pistols reminiscent of the days of duels; dulcimers made of polished black walnut.

Each was a museum piece. One of the rifles hung in the office of Kentucky Governor Ned Breathitt; another was a gift to President Lyndon B. Johnson.

When Dixon's ancestors settled in Letcher County in 1805, only rich men owned Kentucky long rifles like those he makes, and sometimes a man would trade a farm to get one.

"I make every gun like it was the last one I'll ever get a chance at," he told me. "Sometimes it takes over a month to get all the grain sanded and polished just so. I don't make any money on it. The real pleasure is watching a man's face when he picks it up for the first time."

Judge Dixon places a small silver plate on each rifle he makes, recording the date it was completed and the name of the new owner. By now his guns and dulcimers can be found from New York to California, and as far away as London and Korea.

The judge said he had never advertised, and that he didn't want any more orders. "I've got enough to keep me busy for four years," he said. "I'm 75 years old, and I'll probably not be able to fill the orders I have on file now."

I begged to be added to the waiting list. He agreed reluctantly. "Chances are I'll never get around to doing it," he said. "A man can only do so much."

Trading Day brings to town the guns, mules, coon dogs, produce, and almost every other necessity and near-necessity of mountain life. In Norton, Virginia, it has happened every Wednesday for some 35 years.

By 7:30 a.m. at least 150 mud-caked cars and pickups displaying assorted wares crowded the bartering area between the Bargain Barn Sewing Center and the Church of God. Scores more lined the highway nearby.

Bartering is a mountain custom dating back to Appalachia's earliest settlers. "They'll trade about anything you'd ever want here," a miner said. "Knives, horses, bottles, saddles, guns, potatoes, onions, pots, butter churns, antiques, junk—anything."

Almost everyone had two or three guns: pistols tucked under their belts or holstered to their sides, shotguns and rifles slung over shoulders.

Daniel Beverly of Wise, Virginia, had set up shop on the tailgate of his green pickup. His wares included seven high-powered rifles, a .38-caliber pistol, and a pocket watch.

"We're just a bunch of country people having fun," he said. "Been comin' here every week for the last 35 years. Not for money, just for fun; seein' your friends, sometimes people you haven't seen in years. You can get most anything you want here about half price, and it'll do you as good as anything store-bought."

A middle-aged man in a leather vest had been eyeing one of the rifles on the truck bed. Now, without saying a word, he held out a .38 Smith & Wesson revolver. Beverly took it, examined it, twirled the cylinder. "Have to have a little to boot," he said.

The man reached out for the rifle and inspected it carefully. Finally he took $15 from his wallet, still without speaking. Beverly accepted the money, and the firearms changed hands. The man walked off toward another truck.

"That's how it's done," Beverly said, fingering his salt-and-pepper mustache. "You just done saw yourself a trade."

John Patterson, a short, heavyset man from Cranks, Kentucky, was puffing. He had just loaded a small black pony into his pickup. He grinned as he admired the pony and a hog beside it. "Swapped a dog and a lawn mower for 'em," he said.

Forty yards away, a man from Cooper Ridge was disappointed. A tan pony grazed beside his pickup. "What I had in mind was swapping for a workhorse. But there ain't none here," he said.

Later when I had returned to Dan Beverly's pickup, I made the mistake of asking him if receipts were given to record trades. He laughed. "Us hillbillies don't need no receipts. What you get is your receipt. If you trade with a man, you know him. His word is his bond. We don't have those crooks around here."

*O*n a wet Saturday several weeks later, George Wooten waited for a tardy defendant in his austere courtroom in Hyden, Kentucky.

"I cut up 57 moonshine stills in this county when I was sheriff," he was telling two U. S. forest rangers. "Greatest mistake I ever made. Moonshine used to be a way of life—the only free enterprise system we had in these mountains."

Wooten, a dark, blustery man of 56, holds one of the most demanding jobs in American politics. He's judge of Leslie County, one of Appalachia's poorest "—but rich in people and potential." As judge, he has—in addition to his judicial duties—the responsibilities of chief executive. In a small, remote place like Leslie County, government is pretty much what he says it is. Thus, whenever a problem arises—a neighborhood feud, a bridge washout, a late welfare check, a grave to be dug—someone calls George Wooten. An astute politician, he responds with whatever help he can muster, sometimes climbing aboard a bulldozer to grade a road after other county employees have gone home.

It is a grueling, 16-hour-a-day job. The pay is poor. The problems that parade before him daily—deprivation, environmental ruin, isolation—are almost insurmountable. The means to deal with them are meager. Yet Judge Wooten remains optimistic about what he sees as the area's opportunities.

Law and order as practiced in his courtroom are informal. "I hardly ever have a lawyer in here on these misdemeanor cases," he told me. "Mostly we talk cases out, and generally harmonize them. Ninety-nine percent of the trouble in this world could be solved if people would just talk their problems out."

The first defendant, a lean, bedraggled man of 23 from Greasy Creek, arrived at 10:30 a.m., an hour after his case was scheduled to be heard.

Staff member Karen Cox interviews Mrs. Grover Bradley, a lifelong resident of Rabun Gap, Georgia, for the student quarterly "Foxfire." In 1966 a young teacher challenged his students to publish a magazine. The highly successful result records memories, folklore, and craft techniques of mountain people.

"Albert, what you charged with?" Judge Wooten asked.

"Settin' fire."

"Settin' a fire is a real serious offense. How much education you got?"

After a long silence, Albert slowly raised his chin off his chest and muttered, "Reckon none."

"You know in any case you've got your rights," Wooten continued in a grandfatherly tone. "What we're trying to do is prevent fires and save our timber. Of course, you're supposed to have an attorney. If you want you can hire one, or we can appoint you one—or we can just talk it out."

Everyone agreed to talk it out. After 20 minutes, Albert pledged to help the Forest Service fight any fire that might come up in his area, and to try to scrape together some money to repay the fire fighters who extinguished the 80-acre blaze that somehow started on his place. The forest rangers weren't totally satisfied, but they shook Wooten's hand. "If we were sure it was set intentionally, judge, we'd push it harder," the senior officer said. "This fire has happened. We want to stop the next one."

"Good public relations is the key to that," the judge answered.

In like fashion, Wooten disposed of each of the other cases that came up. Court was over in 90 minutes, but not before he had lectured two teen-agers suspected of stealing electrical equipment; consoled a mother who said her youngest son was "full of meanness"; and promised to "make us a peace" between two feuding families.

Justice had been served. Yet not a single lawyer, policeman, or bondsman had been inside the courtroom. No fine or prison term had been levied. The two teen-age suspects were released after their parents agreed to bring them back before the county grand jury. There was no bail bond; again, a man's word was his bond.

"You don't need a jury to have county court," Wooten said. "I believe I can judge any case about as good as a juryman, and save him having to come in for the $1 a day we can pay him."

That afternoon we set out to visit Wooten's boyhood home—Hell for Certain Creek—in an open, war-surplus jeep. Tradition says the creek gained its name when a group of pioneer hunters decided that the desolate, rugged terrain "must be hell for certain."

During the next four hours our jeep forded rivers and creek beds, bounced up rain-slicked hillsides, and at one point got mired axle-deep in clay mud. Two weeks of rain had washed away what little gravel had covered the one-lane roads, and they were badly in need of work.

At every house and homestead we visited, Wooten—part hill-country farmer, part tour guide, part progressive county executive, part braggart—enjoyed himself as only a confident politician can. He kissed babies, viewed farmers' crops, hugged elderly women, joked with teenagers, and sipped moonshine whiskey with some old friends in the remote hills.

Many Appalachian politicians are suspicious of journalists, and resent the publicity the region's poverty has received in recent decades. Not Wooten; he was completely candid with me. "I'm proud, but not too proud to see the needs here," he said as we passed a shanty.

Besides, the publicity has brought millions of dollars in War on Poverty funds into every county in southern Appalachia. Unfortunately the money has done little to improve the basic fabric of life there, and in many cases has left the poor disillusioned; still, it has bandaged some of the wounds of neglect. Wooten takes great satisfaction in the fact that a new highway, paid for partially by the Appalachian Regional Commission, will soon open up the county to visitors; that he's been able to grade countless miles of road and build hundreds of bridges and 15 roadside parks with federal grants; that the county has a new library and water system; that a new $3,000,000

(Continued on page 62)

Taking a break from tinkering with their cars, amateur mechanics relax beside a Confederate battle flag on a porch near Harlan, Kentucky. Many young people have left their mountain communities because of a chronic shortage of job opportunities.

58

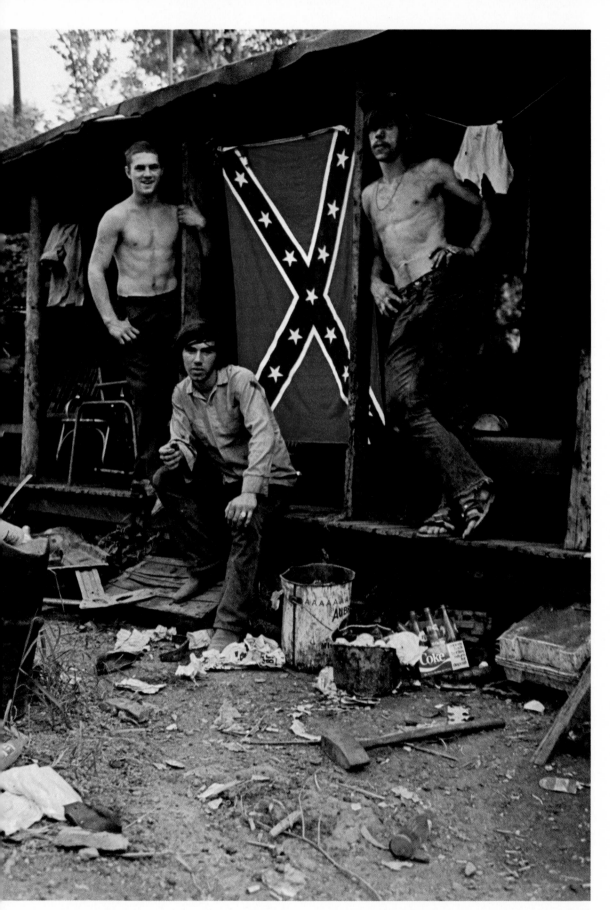

Spitting defiance, a raccoon at bay
defends its precarious perch on a
moored log during coon dog trials
near London, Kentucky. Each dog
has three minutes to topple the coon
into the pond; men in a boat then
quickly haul the dog aboard, to
prevent further damage to either
animal. At top, dogs strain at their
leashes, then plunge into the water
for the trials' swimming race. A
raccoon in a suspended cage, pulled
across the pond, lures the dogs the
300 feet. Other events test the
dogs' tracking and treeing abilities.
Competition takes place one Sunday of
each summer month in many southern
mountain areas. At London, the money
raised goes to restock the nearby
woods with raccoons; in 1973 the
Laurel County Coon Club planned to
import 400 from Florida at $7 a head.

general hospital is under construction.

The homes along Hell for Certain are few and far between. Those we visited contained plain-talking, hardworking country farmers; people not afraid to embrace a friend, not ashamed to be called hillbillies. Three of them invited us to stay for dinner.

At the head of Devil's Jump Branch, Wooten skidded the jeep to a halt. We had driven nearly ten minutes through solid forest, pitching from one side of the roller-coaster road to another, and the pause was welcome. The drizzle had turned to driving rain, and I sat half-soaked under a paint-splattered tarp.

The judge shoved his baseball cap back on his head. "This is happy country," he said. "I think we've got a hidden treasure here if we can preserve our natural beauty and way of life. We're rich and don't even know it."

The final stop of the day was at Russell Sandlin's place. He had just returned from a daylong fishing trip. "Goin' to have some fish, ain't you?" he yelled.

Inside, Rose Sandlin was heating grease in a heavy skillet. Wooten pitched in, rolling the fish in a flour-and-salt mixture, then placing them in the sizzling fat. By the time the fish and two skillets of corn biscuits were ready, four more men had dropped by, one of them a former state senator.

We ate eagerly, but almost in silence. Eating is serious business in the mountains, not to be interrupted with too much conversation. Mrs. Sandlin presided with a warm smile. As we finished, two more visitors showed up. She greeted them and kept on cooking.

*E*astward across the mountains lie the coalfields: the grimy mining camps with quaint names like Marrowbone and Lookout in Kentucky, Slab Fork and Landgraff in West Virginia, and dozens more; the long lines of railroad cars heaped high with "black gold"; the smoldering slag heaps; and the scores of miners with crippled bodies.

Bill Carroll is one of the miners.

You can find him almost any day sitting on an old church pew—dubbed the "black-lung bench"—beside Elmore's service station in Cabin Creek, West Virginia, site of some of the fiercest battles in the history of the American labor movement.

Carroll, slow-talking father of seven, is among an estimated 100,000 miners and former miners who suffer from black lung, or coal-miner's pneumoconiosis. Until March 21, 1972, when he experienced a "suffocating spell" on the job, he was a loading-machine operator for the Cannelton Coal Company 17 miles from his home.

"It had been bothering me for two years, but I kept forcing myself to work," he recounted. "Then in March, I began taking suffocating spells. It seems like you're breathing OK but it don't do no good. You take a sweat. You get all shaking and nervous, and you just can't do nothing with yourself."

Carroll somehow managed to hobble out of the mine on his own power, but the doctor told him, "Your working days are over."

Coal miners accept such pronouncements with impassive fatalism. Their occupation is the nation's most hazardous: four times as dangerous as trucking; two and a half times as perilous as logging. One miner in 12 who enters a mine as a young man can expect to be killed before he reaches retirement. In 1971 alone, 180 men died and 11,380 were injured in the pits.

"I'd say I'm one of the lucky ones," Bill Carroll said. "I always tried to be safe." He's never been seriously injured in a mine accident. His limbs are intact. And he harbors no ill will toward Cannelton Coal: "It's as good a coal company as you'll find in the Kanawha Valley. They care about men, not just coal.

"I'd like to keep working. Of course, you rate a miner like a mule. He's kind of a brute to start with."

But at age 57, Bill Carroll knows there's little chance of working again. His breath grows short even walking across a room. He can't climb a hill or mow a lawn. Sleep comes hard, and often he wakes up coughing. "It won't get no better, the doctors say. You take it easy and you live a little longer."

There are many such men in the dingy, half-deserted coal camps that cluster the length of Cabin Creek. Most of them live in houses grown dark with age and coal dust, built in the days when mining companies owned all the land, paid their workers in scrip good only at the company stores, and exploited them in numerous other ways.

The practices of those years left a heritage of anger and despair. On Cabin Creek, the coal diggers struck back in two bloody labor wars.

In the spring of 1912, nearly 7,500 miners walked off their jobs, demanding union recognition and a fair day's wage. Mine owners retaliated by throwing the strikers out of company-owned houses, importing hundreds of armed men, and building concrete pillboxes fortified with machine guns beside their mine entrances. Ill-fed and ill-clothed, miners' families set up housekeeping in ragged tent cities while gradually arming themselves. The impasse lasted almost a year. At least 50 men died in shoot-outs, and martial law was declared three times.

Discontent survived the uneasy settlement. Not quite eight years later, Cabin Creek men joined an armed march toward Logan County in southwestern West Virginia. More than 3,000 miners, identified by red neckerchiefs, met an even larger and better equipped army of company guards and state police on rugged Blair Mountain. For two days machine guns barked, airplanes dropped crude bombs on the miners, and a never-determined number of men died before Regular Army troops broke up the battle.

The mine wars brought precious few victories, and it was not until the days of President Franklin D. Roosevelt that miners gained full union recognition. But even thereafter coal continued to take its toll on the people and on the land. Eventually the United Mine Workers themselves became bitterly divided; in the union's 1972 election, rebellious reformers won a close victory.

Carroll strongly supports the reform movement. One reason is his sons; he'd

Appalachian moonshiner trudges through the woods carrying a "thumping keg" — part of the apparatus for his still — and a jar containing some of his product. Illicit mountain distillers, steadily decreasing, now usually supply only themselves and a few trusted customers.

like to see their jobs made safer. Carroll has three of them in the pits. All became miners over his strong objections.

But, said Willis Carroll, 23, "I went up to Cleveland and tried to work." He was sipping black coffee in his mother's immaculate kitchen. "I wasn't satisfied, so I came back. People seemed different up there. They didn't want to associate with mountain people.

"Now I'm a coal miner. Guess I'll always be. Wouldn't want to work at anything else now."

His father shook his head. "Wait till you get that dust on your lungs," he said.

Willis crossed the room for more coffee. Many of his contemporaries, he acknowledged, want nothing to do with an industry as dangerous and unpredictable as coal. But he wants to remain where he grew up, and he wants to work underground. Miners make about $42 a day; few other jobs in the coalfields pay more than $2 an hour. And there's something about working underground, close to the earth, that appeals to his sense of masculinity and mountain pride.

"I always wanted to go in the mines to find out what it's like," he said. "It gets rough sometimes. You have to get rough with it. It's exciting work that takes a lot more skill than you think. It keeps your mind occupied.

"Mom didn't want me to go in, of course. She's always scared until I come home at night."

Bill and Willis Carroll, along with all the other coal miners, know why. That same day, Bethlehem Mines Corporation's No. 111 at Kayford was not operating. A slate fall at 10:15 the previous evening had killed Beecher Robinson, Sr., 64, of nearby Acme. He was only weeks from retirement. His wife and nine grown children survived him.

News of disaster spreads like brushfire through coal camps, and by morning everyone on Cabin Creek knew that the miners, observing the practice customary after a fatality, weren't working at Kayford. Late that afternoon I visited Acme, an old company-built town with a boarded-up school. Intermingled with the sorrow, I found, was a matter-of-fact reaction characteristic of coal miners.

One invited me into his house trailer. Robinson had once lived next door to him, and they worked the same shift at Kayford. "That old man was practically like a brother to me," he said.

The miner's wife, worn-looking at 26, nodded. She had heard the ambulance go by in the night. "When my husband came home and I saw it wasn't him, I was crying and I grabbed him around the neck. I feel for that man's family. I lost my dad and uncle both the same way."

She was almost in tears. When she recovered, she added, "If you're married to a miner you don't ever know when your husband's coming home, or when you'll be alone."

Earlier that day she had visited one of Robinson's daughters. They had wept and prayed together.

"I told her, 'God decided your daddy's time had come.' She told me he wasn't afraid to go."

The miner had listened in silence. Now he bowed his head. "Each and every man has a time and a way to go," he said. "When your time is up you go. Every miner knows that."

This same fatalism, coupled with traditional mountain independence, has bred a religion of bedrock fundamentalism laced with superstition. It's a highly personal faith that accepts hardship, disappointment, and failure on this earth as almost inevitable, and emphasizes the hereafter. It's a religion that has shaped and been shaped by mountain life.

A straight-back pew in one of the tiny, white wooden churches that dot the hillsides of every mountain community is the best place to observe it. For generations these churches most often were Baptist, sometimes Methodist. Their ministers tended to be uneducated, plain-talking men who were farmers or storekeepers during the week, preachers on Sunday. But in recent decades other denominations—Holiness, Pentecostal—have sprung up with a sterner yet more emotional style of worship that includes speaking in tongues, faith healing, and—

(Continued on page 80)

Miner Walter Brown, Jr., helps operate a coal auger.

COAL MINING—both boon and curse of the
southern Appalachians—leaves its mark on
men and land alike. Coal is the region's principal employer, and miners are well paid; but
their jobs are not only hazardous but also un-
certain, for mechanized efficiency has greatly
reduced the requirement for labor.

Surface mining now accounts for half the
nation's coal. Bulldozers or power shovels
gouge out the black seams after stripping off
as much as a hundred feet of overlying earth,
or "overburden." Huge, extendable augers
bore horizontally into hillsides, pulling out
coal as they turn. The new methods have
caused deep scarring and erosion of land, and
pollution of air and water.

Thousands of miners still work underground, reaching the coal face by long tunnels or vertical shafts. Why did these men
become—and remain—miners, risking lung
ailments, crippling accidents, and death?
West Virginian William Sheme, 57, sums it
up this way: "A lot of people say mining is all
we know, but it's not that. I've worked in steel
mills and in auto plants, and I've spent 25
years in the mines. And there you've got to be
a skilled man." Miners take pride in their
work—as many of them testify with bumper

Green hills of Kentucky: To get to the coal, strip miners scrape off the natural cover and cut terraces, dumping the waste downhill or into an earlier cut. The devastated area above—about 40 miles north of Harlan—typifies Kentucky's 110,000 acres of abandoned, or "orphan," mines. At left, bulldozers strip a hilltop near Manchester down to a layer of coal. A 1966 Kentucky law made strip mine operators responsible for restoring the approximate original contours of the land and replanting 70 percent of the surface. Conservationists continue to press for a halt to strip mining; mine workers urge strong enforcement of the 1966 law, arguing that the region needs both mine and land-reclamation jobs to combat its severe unemployment.

Walter Brown and crew wait for a truck to load. After boring into a seam, they disconnect the

rig from the embedded auger, back off, fit one of the extra auger lengths, and resume drilling.

Going on shift at Robinson Run No. 95,
miners aboard an electric personnel
carrier, or "jeep," start their trip toward
the section where they will spend the
day 350 feet underground. The West
Virginia mine, a property of Consolida-
tion Coal Company, opened in 1967;
in early 1973 it employed 470 men
who worked in three shifts five days a
week. Opposite, above, a miner's
battery-operated lamp—his only light
source—plays on a five-foot bolt
driven through several layers of rock
to anchor in solid limestone and hold up
the coal ceiling, in lieu of a timber
support. At right, another miner
coats exposed surfaces with powdered
limestone to cover the highly combustible
coal dust that steadily accumulates,
thus reducing the danger of ignition.

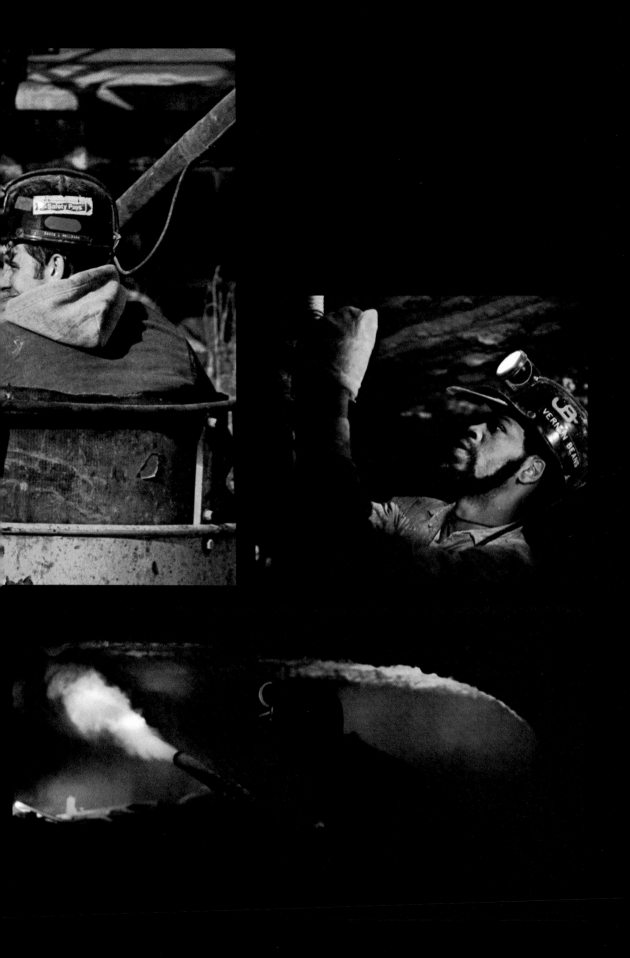

Headlight of a personnel carrier illuminates rails and walls ahead as miners

roll through a six-mile tunnel to the working section of Robinson Run No. 95.

Aboveground again, the miners greet the daylight, swinging lunch buckets that hold both food trays and drinking water. The rearmost man in center carries a safety lamp; its naphtha flame lengthens in the presence of methane, a gas that seeps out of coal seams and, in concentration, is dangerously explosive. In the changing room, opposite, the men hang clothes on basket hooks they can raise and lower by wires. Lingering in the warm spray, below, a miner washes off the day's grime. Workers at mines that have no showers receive "soap money" of 30 cents a day.

Coal-camp houses crowd the trackside
at Concrete Springs, West Virginia.
Mining companies used to build entire
towns, requiring workers to rent the
houses and to buy all goods at a company
store. Former miner Bill Carroll
(opposite) occupied one of the Concrete
Springs houses for 12 years. Disabled
since early 1972, the 57-year-old
Carroll now lives nearby; he suffers
from black lung, an ailment common to
miners who must work in fine coal dust.
"After your lungs get in bad shape,
it's even hard to get shed of a cold,"
Carroll says. "So I just lay around the
house, hardly go anywhere anymore."

Saving hugs and kisses for later, Sissy, 4, and Bobby, 2, join their daddy, Willis Carroll, on the front porch after he arrives home from work. Willis, 23, drives a shuttle car, moving coal through the tunnels of Cannelton Coal Company's Mine No. 115 near Montgomery, West Virginia. He went into the mine when he was 18, showing no hesitation about taking up the kind of work that ruined his father's health. Bill Carroll tried to dissuade Willis, but concedes, "Conditions in the mines now are 90 percent better than when I started putting in my 31 years."

in rare cases — even snake handling as an expression of God's will.

The congregation gathered early outside the Mozelle Church of God. Teenagers strolled in clusters; old men kicked at the dust with their high-topped shoes. "Not much to do here except go to church," my friend Vance Mosley commented as we waited for the service to begin one Saturday night in mid-May.

At 6:15 p.m. the Reverend Carlo Caldwell hobbled out of his small white cottage on a hill a quarter mile away. He walked with a stoop, a hand-carved hickory cane in one hand. Vance watched uneasily. He attended this church until he was 13, when a neighborhood feud split the congregation. He hadn't been back in almost 20 years.

"Glad to have you here. No matter what you come for," Preacher Caldwell said when he saw us. "You know, though, we preach the truth. Not like some of those preachers always talking about what's happening in New York and such."

He limped into the church, stopping on the steps to kiss a small girl. Inside he went from pew to pew shaking each worshiper's hand. A small portrait of Christ looked out from behind the pulpit. Nearby on the wall hung a clock donated by Chappell's Dairy.

Soon 34 people were sitting in the varnished pews: men on one side, women — some with babes in their arms — on the other. Among the men there wasn't a necktie or coat. Women wore no makeup, and their uncut hair was pulled straight back from the forehead; their plain cotton dresses reached well below the knee.

Sister Ruth Roark opened the service with a hymn. She was accompanied by her own guitar, two electric guitars, a set of drums, a piano, and a tambourine. The music filled the tiny room with fervor, and there was much tapping of feet. Gradually other voices joined in, singers stepping forward to the pulpit in turn for brief solos or duets. Everyone sang from memory.

Their voices were loud and unabashed. Their songs — partly hill-country ballads, partly gospel hymns — echoed into the evening for almost an hour.

Then came the prayers. Worshipers dropped to their knees and began speaking in tongues. The muted, mumbling sounds rose and faded, filling the church with emotion, finally ending in a relief of silence.

Dusk had fallen by the time Preacher Caldwell, thin and infirm, stepped to the pulpit. "I never know when I'll preach my last sermon," he said. His collar was open. His blue sweater hung from a nail on the wall. "I'm 73 years old and weak in the body."

But his voice quickly gathered momentum. "People have let the fire go out," he declared. "They like to sit still. Benchwarmers, that's what I call them. I tell you, you're not going to be saved by warming a bench. You're going to have to be reborn."

"Hallelujah!" someone shouted near the front. "Glory be to God!"

"When you believe in the power of God, you begin to shout and shake," Preacher Caldwell continued. His arms shot up, quivering. "Hallelujah! Hallelujah! I'm beginning to get moving. I'm beginning to feel the Lord.

"Brothers and sisters, it's great to follow Jesus," he said. "It's the greatest thing anyone can do."

Later there were testimonies, and finally an altar call.

"The Lord has a lot of good things for us. The devil ain't got nothing but a bin of fire. Do you know you could die tonight?" Preacher Caldwell asked, looking at Vance and me. "If you died tonight, where would your soul go? To the glories of heaven or to the fires of hell?"

On a hillside not far from Harlan, Kentucky, another Holiness church — the Pine Mountain Church of God — struggles to keep alive one of the most bizarre mountain religious practices: snake handling. The Reverend K. D. Browning, a 76-year-old retired candy salesman, has been the church's pastor for more than 40 years.

"It's dangerous, oh, it's dangerous," he says. "In a few years there won't be nobody doing it. People just aren't believing in it any more."

The belief and the snakes, however, are still very much alive at the Pine Mountain church. One evening in early summer, Vance Mosley and I sat in a back pew and waited until Brother Dexter Callahan arrived with two small, screened cages. He placed them under a bench near the pulpit.

Suddenly the tiny church was alive with prayer and thanksgiving. The congregation dropped to its knees, voices rising in a shrill, unintelligible chorus. In a moment it ended; then Preacher Browning's wife worked the worshipers into a frenzied chant, clapping her hands, pacing back and forth: "Glory, praise the Lord! I'll be singing tonight.... Glory, praise the Lord! There'll be preaching tonight. There'll be preaching tonight."

The members stood, elbow to elbow, in a large square around the pulpit: men on one half of the square, women on the other. Mrs. Browning's chant continued. Hands clapped. Bill Huff, a quarry worker and snake hunter, gently struck cymbals to the beat. Someone strummed a guitar. A child shook a tambourine, adding to the driving rhythm.

Morning frost spins a delicate web on the ribbed leaf of a blackberry bush in the mountains of West Virginia.

Tension grew as the sounds filled the tiny room and spilled out into the night. Here and there a member "got the Spirit"; shoulders shook, arms flailed heavenward. One middle-aged woman stood beside a portrait of Christ, speaking in tongues, her head shaking violently. I looked at Brother Dexter, who appeared to go into a self-induced trance; his thick shoulders quivered, his head jerked. His entire body shook to the rhythm of the chant as he opened the snake box and brought out three large copperheads in one hand.

"Praise the Lord, praise the Lord," he said, moving toward the pulpit. He shifted one fat, dark copperhead from his right to his left hand, then passed it to Mrs. Browning. He passed the two remaining snakes to Preacher Browning and another worshiper, and retrieved three more copperheads from the cage.

The sanctuary pulsated to the hard, driving beat. Feet tapped. Knees bent. Worshipers moved back and forth across the room in a weaving, jerky movement that resembled a dance. The serpents' heads swayed this way and that, their forked tongues darting, their tails wrapped around the hands of the faithful.

It ended as suddenly as it began. Preacher Browning, a sturdy, bald-headed man in a plaid shirt, advanced to the pulpit. Brother Dexter placed the copperheads back in the box.

"The Bible, it says that they shall pick up poisonous serpents and they who believe shall not be harmed," the preacher proclaimed. "It says they can drink poison and shall not be harmed. It says they shall hold fire and not be burned."

Preacher Browning's sermon continued for the next 90 minutes. His language was plain, his message rooted in common-sense terms. Throughout there was a strong mistrust of organized religion, of seminary-trained preachers, of education, of material wealth.

"I tell you, pride and material things have about taken all the believers," he declared, holding a Bible aloft. "It has to be a meek class of people for the Holy Spirit to work in. . . . If we study in a seminary, we come out preachers. But that doesn't mean we've got the Spirit. . . . John the Baptist didn't study in no seminary. He came out of the wilderness."

Older children and menfolk—miners, farmers, mechanics, storekeepers—wandered outside every now and again, then strolled back to their seats. The women —housewives, mothers, and at least one schoolteacher—sat stoically in place, occasionally tending a child.

After the sermon came songs, more prayers, and testimonies. Then pews and benches filled as the congregation broke into a final chant. Expectations were high, for sometimes the snakes are brought out a second time. No other creature commands the fear and respect that snakes arouse in mountain people, and almost every family has an awesome tale about an encounter with a poisonous serpent. Handling them is a sure-fire attraction—it defies nature. The danger is very real. According to Preacher Browning, Dexter Callahan has been bitten almost a dozen times over the years, and in 1940 a man died from a snakebite he suffered in the Pine Mountain Church of God—evidence to his friends that he must not have had sufficient faith in the promise of safety.

But this night the snakes remained caged. As the chanting mounted, however, a small kerosene torch was brought forward. An elderly man in a blue shirt, who had been silent the entire service, thrust his hand into the foot-high flame, slowly turning it in the heat for a full minute. He showed no pain. Brother Dexter and Mrs. Browning then did the same thing.

Preacher Browning, straight and confident, addressed his closing remarks to the back pew.

"There's people who see this and don't believe it," he said. "If you think this flame is artificial, come up and stick your hand in it. If you think these snakes aren't poisonous, come up and stick your hand in their cage."

Neither Vance nor I took up the pastor's challenge.

*T*he hard times and the hills have instilled a quiet, polite serenity in the old people. Mrs. Matilda (Tildy) Peck is the finest quilt maker I ever met. John Conley is a blacksmith who still opens his shop at 7:30 a.m., rain, snow, or shine. They live hundreds of miles apart: Mrs. Peck in Campton, Kentucky; John Conley in Otto, North Carolina. They have never met, but they share a common heritage, and a mutual distrust of what "progress" has done to the mountains.

Tildy Peck seldom had time for needlework when her family of six children and two stepchildren was growing up. She would rise at 4 a.m., fix breakfast, then head for the fields with her hoe. "I'd work out there all day," she told me one afternoon in her bright sewing room, where a picture of Woodrow Wilson hangs on the wall. "Never was much to get tired. In April or May I'd always shed my shoes. Did ever since I was a child, whenever the weather would get warm."

The Pecks' rented hillsides yielded the barest of crops. "About enough to feed our horse and cow and make some cornbread out of the rest of it," Tildy said.

She continued working in the fields well past her 65th birthday, and kept right on canning sweet corn, beans, tomatoes, and cucumbers.

"I always could use my hands pretty good." Tildy folded her long, slender fingers across her lap. Her gray-white hair was pulled back in a neat bun. "Never did quilt much, exceptin' what we used. Once in a while I'd sew for a friend. They'd buy the material and I'd make 'em a quilt for a dollar and a half."

Now Tildy sews almost every day, spending up to a month on each of the fine quilts she sells (underpriced, I am convinced) for up to $90 to a self-help cooperative, the Grass Roots Craftsmen of the Appalachian Mountains, in Jackson, Kentucky. They are works of art—exact, intricate stitches shaping bright, handsome patterns.

Many of her 86 years seem to pass from Tildy's thin face as she stacks samples of her work atop her bed, explaining the pattern of each quilt. Her blue eyes dance.

"I enjoy quiltin'," she said. "Last one I did, I almost had a heart attack. Let up on it awhile, but I'm startin' again. I can't hardly sit and do nothing. I think anyone is better workin' than idlin' around. It prolongs your days if you use 'em right."

Her eyes turned to the window and a granddaughter working in the garden below the farmhouse. "It would be a pretty good idea if some of the young folks took up quiltin'," she said. "Us old people won't be here always to make 'em."

A heavy morning fog shrouded the J. N. Conley General Repair and Welding Shop the day photographer Bruce Dale and I visited. It was not yet eight o'clock, but Conley was hammering away at a wheelbarrow.

"I repair everything in here from bulldozers on down," he said. "Young fellows don't seem to want to fool with repairing anymore. Lot of them don't want to work nohow."

It wasn't always that way in the Carolina hills. When Conley was growing up, he said, a man took pride in what he could produce with his hands. His father was a carpenter and cabinetmaker. But

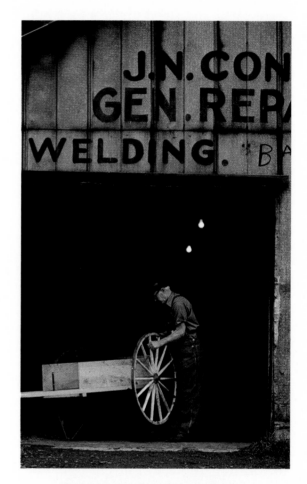

Blacksmith and repairman for 55 years, J. N. Conley of Otto, North Carolina, began his career shoeing horses and fixing wagons, later turning to farm machinery and automobiles. Nowadays he works mostly on bicycles, wheelbarrows, and lawn mowers.

when John went to work in 1918, at the age of 16, he wanted to be a blacksmith.

Smiths were known for being truthful and honest, he explained. "They said a blacksmith always pays his debts." Conley has tried to live by that credo. "I don't hold anyone up even if they have a million dollars."

He crossed his dark shop, crowded with a lifetime's collection of tools and spare parts, and stood under a bare light bulb looking at the cold ashes in his forge. "Truthfulness and honesty—best religion I ever had," he said.

Conley is a small man with thick forearms. He wears black horn-rimmed glasses, and bib overalls soiled by grease and wear; a small cap covers his head.

The years, of course, have wrought vast changes on John Conley and his work. When he started as a blacksmith, he spent much of his time shoeing horses. He also built wagons, from the wheels up. As the years passed, he learned to repair autos, and became expert on farm equipment. He added an arc welder to his electric drills and lathes and saws.

Today, many of the old farmers have retired and real estate developers have bought their land for vacation homes, ski lodges, and tourist havens. Outsiders have flooded in, changing mountain life and contributing little to Conley's shop other than broken lawn mowers.

There's still plenty of work for the old blacksmith, however—and he wishes he could find a young assistant to whom he could pass on his trade. "I'm going to stay with it as long as I'm able," he said. "Wouldn't have nothing else to do."

*M*any ponder the plight of the southern Appalachians. Scholars fret about the future of the mountaineer. Folklorists and romantics devise schemes to preserve his past. Bureaucrats plot how to put food in his stomach and bring progress to his hills. But Rabun Gap, Georgia, is one of the few places where anyone is trying to find out what mountaineers themselves—especially the old people—have to say and to offer. Surprisingly enough, it's a group of teen-agers that is doing the listening.

It started in 1966 when Eliot Wigginton, fresh out of graduate school at Cornell, found his classroom in disarray after only six weeks as an English teacher at Rabun Gap-Nacoochee School. The students were bored. Discipline was in shambles. In desperation, he walked into class one morning and asked, "How would you like to throw away the text and start a magazine?"

The result has been a highly readable quarterly called *Foxfire*, written, edited, and illustrated by high-school students. Much of the material has been republished in a best-selling book. *Foxfire's* subject matter is the mountain life around Rabun Gap—"hog dressing, log cabin building, mountain crafts and foods, planting by the signs, snake lore, hunting tales, faith healing, moonshining, and other affairs of plain living." The sources of information are the grandparents, the great-aunts and great-uncles, and the older neighbors of the students.

Blacksmith John Conley is one. Five youngsters spent days watching him build a wagon wheel, asking questions, photographing his work, and marveling at his skill. Stan Echols of Clayton, Georgia, was particularly impressed when Conley stayed up half the night to redo much of the wheel because he'd made a slight mistake: "He didn't want anything imperfect to leave his shop."

Another teacher has dedicated his life to seeing that the newest generation of mountaineers should not forget its heritage. For 24 years Harding Ison has been teaching grades one through eight at Kingdom Come in one of eastern Kentucky's last one-room schools.

It was built in 1915 or 1917, depending on which local historian you listen to, and its walls show its age; but it sits in an almost unblemished vale. Beside it bubbles Kingdom Come Creek, chock full of crawdads, hornyheads, and jackfish, much as it was 80 years ago when John Fox, Jr., visited the hollow before writing the mountain classic *The Little Shepherd of Kingdom Come*.

Ison, a short, crew-cut bachelor of 49, has had many chances to leave for a better job. But he stays in the same building where he and his 12 brothers and sisters learned their ABC's—teaching a handful of students each year, hoping that Kingdom Come will never lose its school.

"I'm kind of like Robert E. Lee," he told me. "He thought his first duty was to Virginia. My first duty is to Kingdom Come. I don't think a community is a community without a good school and a good church. We've got both."

The school had a stark homeyness. The worn, unpainted floorboards were well-scrubbed. A large potbellied stove burned in the middle of the room. Abraham Lincoln, George Washington, and Douglas MacArthur gazed down solemnly from above the blackboard. A miniature log cabin perched on a ledge. Rocks, bones, tree bark, and sections of a beehive identified a crowded nature corner.

"We've made miners, carpenters, farmers, engineers, mechanics, doctors, and a lawyer—even a few professional fox hunters—right here in this room," Ison said. "It may seem like we don't get as much schooling done, but when it comes to standardized tests the kids from here do as well as or better than the other children in Letcher County."

The atmosphere was free and easy. Students called the teacher by his first name, and wandered about at will. Lessons were direct and uncomplicated; frequently they contained a moral.

"Lincoln grew up to be President with very little formal education," Ison said, sitting on his desk at the center of the room. "But he was a good observer—and he was interested."

Lincoln was born in a log cabin with a dirt floor near Hodgenville, Kentucky, halfway across the state from Kingdom Come. "You can hardly imagine anyone living as they did in the pioneer days. But a lot of men who became great came from poor families. A lot of things don't come easy. That's why we strive."

Seventeen desks stretched out in four rows in front of Ison. The children of Kingdom Come are strikingly beautiful, their faces open and frank, with the fair features of their English, Scottish, and Irish ancestors. While Ison lectured to the older pupils, two first-graders wrote

Half-dovetailing, an intricate method of corner timbering, snugly secures the walls of a log house near Chappell, Kentucky. The structure has withstood wind, snow, and rain for 131 years.

on the blackboard. One named Ronnie passed me a note. "I like you," it said.

Soon it was recess. The older girls strolled down a worn path to a grove 200 yards away. The boys waded into Kingdom Come Creek, swollen by spring rains. Within minutes, fifth-grader Jefferson Hayes rushed up. "Ever see a jackfish?" he said, uncupping his hands ever so slightly to exhibit a minnow. "I ran 'im up under a rock and grabbed 'im. Last week we had a turtle."

Dickie Banks, a redheaded eighth-grader, emerged from a tangle of underbrush proudly holding a sassafras root. "Just clean it off and you can chew it or make tea," he said.

Soon there will be no more one-room schools. No more jackfish at recess. No more notes from shy first-graders. For good or ill, consolidations and population shifts close more country schools each year. Census figures indicate that half a million people left Appalachia during the 1960's. West Virginia alone lost 116,000 residents, eastern Kentucky more than 46,000.

The harsh facts sadden Harding Ison. "Young people just don't stay put any more," he said as he walked back into the school. "There's so many things out in the world. People don't want to stay here in Kingdom Come."

But Dickie Banks, who was beside us, disagreed. "I want to stay right here on this here creek," he said.

*P*reacher Dan Gibson is afraid it's too late to preserve the hills for Dickie Banks's generation. "The timber's gone, the wildlife's gone, and the water's gone," he told me one winter day as we looked across a barren ridge near his home. "I've tried to save what I could, but I hate to think that this is what this country is leaving my grandchildren."

Gibson is one of Appalachia's angry men, a product of the trials, hardships, and destruction of the 1960's. At 89, he is the stereotype old mountaineer: strong and willowy, thin-faced, with a long, arched nose and skin toughened by the mountain wind. A carpenter by trade, he lives in a pleasant cottage on a knoll

above Cockles Trace Branch of Clear Creek, about six miles from Hindman, Kentucky.

"When I came to the creek 20 years ago," he told me, "the hills were still covered with game. Now you can't hear a quail call anywhere."

Gibson blames the change on strip mining, the entirely legal and, in fact, state-sanctioned practice of gouging rich seams of coal from mountainsides with dynamite and bulldozers. He has spent much of the last decade fighting strip miners, in legislative halls and courtrooms and out on the hillsides. At one point he held off bulldozers and a 40-man posse with his squirrel rifle. "This is my strip-mine law," he says, patting the weapon. "Hot lead is the only thing they understand."

When I first met Preacher Dan several years ago, I spent many hours with him. He told me of his deep fundamentalist faith (he has been an ordained Baptist minister since 1926); and he showed me what strip mining has done to the land. As my car slipped and skidded up the muddy roads to the mountains where the strip miners work, and into the valleys around Clear Creek, Lotts Creek, and Troublesome Creek, Gibson had a story for each hillside.

"See that chimney? Used to be a house there," he said. "A slide just pushed it away. At the end of the hollow the runoff from this same strip washed a fellow's basement clear apart.

"That's the Ritchie place. Back in '66, a 'dozer came around the mountain one day and started rolling boulders down the hill. One knocked the porch clear off. The wife, she had to grab the kids and get out right fast."

Recently I revisited Preacher Dan Gibson for the first time in over a year. His eyes were failing, and he had trouble viewing the hillsides. But his voice was clear, and his hatred of strip mining undiminished. We talked a long time in his living room. He was disappointed that the 1972 Kentucky legislature hadn't done anything to limit stripping; as a result, he said, people on Clear Creek and Lotts Creek had decided to take matters into their own hands. "Any man who comes in here with a bulldozer will leave in a box," he said.

After several hours of conversation we walked to a small shed beside the road. There Gibson the carpenter showed me two coffins he'd made for himself and his wife. He said he was ready for death. I asked him how he thought the Almighty would look on his opposition to strip mining.

"It isn't for myself," he said. "It's for children not born yet."

The wind whistled through scrub pines as they buried Mrs. Bessie Lee Engle in the family plot uphill from the Church of the True Living God on Line Fork Creek, near Viper, Kentucky.

Sister Bessie was a deeply religious woman of 68, an ordained minister of the Holiness faith. "One of the finest Christians I ever knew," the Reverend E. B. McGraner said. "Her testimony was such that you couldn't hear it and not be moved."

Her past was deeply rooted in the coalfields of eastern Kentucky where she lived all of her life. She was married to Arnold Engle, a miner, for 48 years. They reared eight children, tilled a huge garden, and canned long shelves of fruits and vegetables. When coal boomed and times were good, the table was full. When coal declined, or when Arnold was laid up after one of three slate falls that left his body brutally mangled, the garden produce helped to stretch a menu of cornbread, gravy, and salt pork.

Sorrow and loneliness filled Sister Bessie's last years. Her husband and three sons, aged 22, 44, and 49, died within 36 months. Her other children had long since moved to the industrial centers of the Midwest and South, and Bessie was left alone on the two-acre homestead. "I want to join your daddy up on that hillside as soon as I can," she told her sons more than once.

Her life centered on the church. She tithed, attended services, taught adult Sunday-school classes, and journeyed from one small mountain congregation to another offering testimony. She was

Nibbling a blade of grass, 11-year-old Helen Odum wanders a path by her home near the headwaters of the Little Doe River in Tennessee.

an inspiration to all. And more than once, it was said, she used her power of prayer to perform an act of healing.

But when death came to Sister Bessie one Friday night in late spring, she was alone in the Appalachian Regional Hospital in Hazard, Kentucky. Although she had been bedridden for a week, she had not permitted hospital officials to notify her family. "She was that way," her only daughter, Nancy Johnson, explained to me. "She didn't want us to worry."

But by 1:30 p.m. on Monday, when the dusty blue hearse arrived at the Church of the True Living God, cars from Ohio, Texas, Virginia, and Indiana lined the roadway, and 130 persons packed the modest sanctuary, designed to hold no more than 75.

Some Appalachian funerals last for several hours, with as many as five ministers officiating. Bessie Engle's was a simple service; it lasted just over an hour, and there were two preachers.

Mr. McGraner spoke first. Mrs. Engle, he said, had instructed him not to eulogize her. "She told me many a time, 'When I die, just pull my body over in front of the pulpit and preach the word of Jesus Christ.'"

Unloosening his bright rose necktie, he promptly ignored her request. Sister Bessie's death, he said, crowned a generous and inspirational life. Her passing "is not a disaster, it is divine. This is not gloom, this is glory. This is not defeat, this is victory. This didn't just happen, it was ordered."

The Reverend Jerry Back, a younger man, spoke with a more restrained eloquence. "Everyone who knew Sister Bessie had to love her," he said. "Our loss is heaven's gain. One of God's best has passed."

He lifted his eyes. "Tell Bessie that we're coming," he said. "We're traveling the footsteps of those who preceded us. Tell her for us, 'We'll meet you in the morning.'"

The coffin was opened at the close of the service. Mrs. Engle looked serene in a crisp pink and white dress. "Mother liked bright, new things," her son Felix, a pipe-fitter from Franklin, Ohio, told

me later. "To the last, her house looked more like newlyweds lived there than an old widow lady."

The mourners filed silently by the coffin, most pausing briefly beside it. Several touched Mrs. Engle's hand in farewell. Preacher Matthew Jackson, who conducted the tent revival 20 years earlier at which Sister Bessie was saved, wept openly. Nancy collapsed across the coffin, sobbing, "Mother. Mother."

They carried Bessie down a well-worn path between two rows of young pines, across Boyd Hall's farmyard, and up the hill. A strong breeze stirred as the procession halted at the burial site. Mr. McGraner bowed his head, his hands clasping a Bible. "There is nothing to worry about," he said. "God has taken Sister Engle home."

In the distance a cock crowed. It was considered a good omen.

A few of us lingered after the coffin was lowered into the ground. What will become of Appalachia, I asked myself, when all the old mountaineers are gone — the James Maggards, the Tildy Pecks, the Dan Gibsons, the Bessie Engles? What will become then of their land and their people?

Felix Engle gave me one answer when I saw him an hour later. The Engle children had scattered to Ohio, Virginia, and Texas years ago, he said. They had their own lives to lead. The old home place would be sold now, the proceeds divided among the heirs.

"There's a drawing power to a mother," he said. "A place never seems the same after you lose her."

Felix paused, then added, "Reckon we won't be back here all together much any more."

But when I returned a week later, the answer had changed. Nancy, Mrs. Engle's youngest child, wore a broad smile. Her four brothers had signed the property over to her, and she was moving her family from Charlottesville, Virginia.

"This is where I belong," she said. "The boys and I couldn't stand to let this place go.

"Now they'll always have a place to come home to."

Hand over her eyes, a woman bows in meditation during an Ozark tent meeting.

"Glory, praise the Lord!"

A FIRM FAITH in God and anticipation of the rewards of the Kingdom of Heaven have sustained many a mountaineer through an austere life. In remote communities of the Appalachians and Ozarks the approach to religion often is fundamentalist, based on a literal interpretation of the King James Version of the Bible. In the 19th century the most successful denominations in both regions were the Baptists and Methodists, with their circuit riders and lay preachers, but in recent decades the Holiness and Pentecostal sects have also become prominent. Even so, the traditional independence of mountain people seems to work against widespread "joinin'." There are far more participants in religious activities than officially enrolled church members.

Yet without question the mountain churches play a vital role. They are social centers, repositories of both gospel and secular music, fountains of inspiration. The intensity of feeling for which hill people are known becomes evident in their worship services—in the music, in the preaching, in the response. For many, these services are central events to which they look forward all week; and they accept eagerly the invitation to "make a joyful noise unto the Lord."

Confirming a spiritual rebirth, the Reverend Perry Fitchue immerses a

convert as others await baptism in Bear Creek near Omaha, Arkansas.

Handling writhing rattlesnakes unharmed, Dexter Callahan of Kentucky's Pine Mountain Church of God demonstrates the strength of his faith. The originator of this ritual, George W. Hensley, in 1909 read the words of Jesus quoted in Mark 16:18 (opposite, below). From then until 1955, when he died of a snakebite, he preached that only true believers should handle poisonous snakes. Below, the Reverend K. D. Browning holds a rattlesnake as confidently as his Bible. In more than 40 years he has lost only one of his Pine Mountain flock to snakebite, although the snakes have struck many. Even Callahan, who supplies the church with both rattlers and copperheads, has suffered nearly a dozen bites. "I got my mind off the Lord," he explains.

Ecstasy of possession by what the congregation recognizes as the Holy Spirit dominates the expression of a young woman at Pine Mountain Church of God. Moments later she burst into a staccato series of unintelligible syllables, reminiscent of Christ's description of the faithful in Mark 16:17: "They shall speak with new tongues." Opposite, an older woman proves her faith through ordeal by fire. Holding a can containing kerosene and a flaming wick, she passes it back and forth beneath her chin with no apparent ill effect. Behind her stands Preacher Browning, who encourages all to take active parts in the services he conducts. A lifelong minister "in response to God's call," he receives no pay; he formerly supported himself as a salesman, and still farms on 20 acres a few miles from the church.

Heeding Christ's exhortation that "they shall lay hands on the sick," Pine Mountain Church members reach out toward an ailing woman in prayer. The worshipers believe the Holy Spirit confers upon them the power to heal by prayer, laying on of hands, and anointing with oil. By touching a man (opposite) possessed of the Holy Spirit, others seek to share in his experience. At left, Preacher Browning—even before removing his hat—embraces a member who has arrived early for one of the weekend's three six-hour services.

Sons and daughters, neighbors and friends
climb to the family graveyard with the
coffin of A. M. Simpson, a Kentucky farmer
who died at the age of 61. Of his ten
children, all except one had left the family
home in Bledsoe, but all returned for
their father's funeral. Opposite, mourners
pay their respects, reminisce quietly,
and comfort one another. Many mountain
people revisit cemeteries on Memorial
Day, still often called Decoration Day;
families bring flowers to the graves and
spend several hours tidying up the grounds.

3

The Ozarks: "I been on this place 84 year"

by Clay Anderson

THE HIGHWAY SOUTH from Gainesville, Missouri, winds along the ridge tops, seeking a line of least resistance as did the trails of the pioneers and, earlier, the paths of the Indians. The roadside oaks part now and then to reveal an endless variety of wooded hills, high meadows and meandering valleys, cedar-scattered glades, and misty, mystic horizons.

The road has become a favorite of mine, not only because it is typical of some of the best of the unspoiled Ozark country but also because it leads to the home of a man unique to these hills.

Just south of the Arkansas line, the road pitches down a knob and into a curve. Make an abrupt right turn across a ditch and you're at Junior Cobb's place.

Metal sheeting that once covered the shanty's exterior walls has been stripped away, exposing scrap planks. The roof is two different shades of tar paper. Two of the three small windows tilt haphazardly; the third is covered with plastic. A crude shop building nearby awaits some covering over the bare studs on one side.

The yard is red dirt, the kind that is powdery when dry and sticky when wet, laced with coarse gravel over formidable outcroppings of ledge rock. Wood shavings, driftwood, and litter are under foot. An old car, its best parts already pirated, is nosed into scrub oaks at the edge of a clearing, near a fishing boat with a disabled motor.

There's not much about the scene to suggest that this is the home of an outstanding artist.

I first learned of Junior Cobb from Peter Engler, a wood-carver himself and proprietor of shops specializing in fine wood products at Reeds Spring and Silver Dollar City, Missouri. Peter has become the patron of a considerable coterie of Ozark carvers, providing them with encouragement, inspiration, and a market that has grown far beyond the bounds of his own shops.

Junior was still a teen-ager when Peter and his mother, Mrs. Ida Engler, discovered the illiterate youngster and his remarkable talent with wood.

He had already sold some carvings, starting with a marionette made in his spare time while helping out on the ferry across the White River south of Mountain Home, Arkansas.

"After I met Pete, I went to whittlin' for him for about two years," Junior told me. "Then I went to just carvin' on my own." Demand soon grew for his relief landscapes and renderings of wildlife and human figures. His wife was a frequent model. "Helen's got Indian blood in her," declares Junior, and he has often depicted her as an Indian maiden in carvings, some of them life-size. Mostly, Junior has only carved in relation to his monetary needs: larger sculptures when he was working on the house, repairing a car, or wanting a gun or a new bow; smaller pieces for day-to-day expenses; quick "whittlin's" for going-to-the-store money.

I met Junior at Ida Engler's gift shop in Lakeview, Arkansas. To keep

Predictable as an Ozark sunrise, the school bus driven by Bill Blair picks up the Hampton children—Danny, Deedee, Dennis, Helen, and Fay—on its 25-mile run to Bradleyville, Missouri, where one building accommodates all 12 grades. Most of the day Bill operates a sawmill business with his father and older son.

him working, she maintained a policy of buying any good carving he brought her. In winter this could cause some financial strain, and to avoid being overstocked with certain kinds of carvings she would offer suggestions; but the results were not necessarily predictable.

"Junior, why don't you carve a hill couple?" she asked one day. The next afternoon he appeared at the shop with a pair of beautifully detailed quail.

His carving seldom takes precedence over hunting, fishing, cave exploring, or digging for Indian artifacts. I found him surprisingly learned in archeology—having spent many hours with scholars he guided to Indian burial sites—and almost mystically in tune with "them people what lived here 7,000 years ago."

After an initial reserve, Junior is open
(Continued on page 112)

As they have for generations, Arkansas youths gather at Sylamore Creek swimming hole on a warm summer afternoon. In February 1973, work began on converting the property into a commercial trailer park that will include 125 campsites, but will retain the swimming hole in its natural state and will leave it open to visitors without charge. The 90-acre park lies six miles from Mountain View, location of a new Folk Cultural Center, and about the same distance from Blanchard Springs Caverns.

Cross-legged on a utility
tractor, the Hamptons'
son Dennis, 17, rests
between farm chores.
His 14-year-old sister
Fay feeds grain to her
pet duck, distinctively
named A Particular Bird.
Later the duck and
several chickens dis-
appeared, presumably
victims of marauding
foxes. At right, a beaming
child of the Ozarks
helps sell apples
from the tailgate of a
pickup truck at roadside.

Morning ritual: Army pensioner
John Caudel, a bachelor in his 70's,
brings neighbor Bill Blair's mail
to him at the sawmill, where he'll
stay awhile to visit. Tenth-grader
Danny Hampton, trailed by the family
dog, Muggins—"kind of a mixed
breed"—sprints past a black walnut
tree on his way to the school bus.
Danny and his brother and sisters
assist their parents with such jobs as
milking and planting. The Hamptons
returned to the Ozarks from the
state of Washington in 1970 and
decided to stay for good on 160 acres
near father Leon's birthplace, where
they raise beef cattle and "just about
anything you can grow in a garden."

Smiling a welcome, Mr. and Mrs. Clarence Capps stand at the gate to their 160-acre farm near Big Clifty Creek, Arkansas. "Some folks call this Capps's Valley," says Mrs. Capps, whose husband's family has lived in the region for generations, "but we call it Whippoorwill Valley. Through the summer the whippoorwills hollo all night long." The couple tend a dairy herd of Holsteins, Jerseys, and Guernseys, as well as chickens and a small truck garden. Mrs. Capps preserves enough tomatoes, beans, peas, and other vegetables for home use, and sells the rest.

"Old-time singing, gladness bringing,
From a lovely land somewhere," sings Judy
Klemmedson of Clinton, Arkansas, as Dude
Black listens. "I love the mountain music
because it's pretty and simple," she says,
"and the people care enough about it to
share it with others." Judy handcrafted the
mountain dulcimer she plays at left, below.
Dude is at home on the guitar, fiddle,
banjo, and mandolin. His mother, Bessie
(opposite), now 79, reared 11 children. "She
knows everything that grows," says Judy,
"and appreciates beauty more than any of us."

and honest with strangers. Well, honest when it matters. His hunting and fishing stories do seem to expand with time, and his treasure-hunting exploits are downright fanciful. Once he told Bruce Dale and me a tale about finding a churn full of gold coins in a plow furrow. He marked the spot with a stick, he said, and went to find out what the coins were "with them little old eagles on the back." But when he came back, the farmer had "crisscross plowed" the field, and the stick was buried with the treasure.

Such stories do little to reinforce Junior's credibility. But it is apparent that he has accumulated no wealth, works mostly to fulfill his immediate needs, and sets his table in large part with fish, game, and other foods of the forest. Until recently there was no water supply on his property; water was hauled in milk cans from a well two miles away. Aside from hunting and fishing equipment, his modern conveniences are a power band saw and a fast-changing collection of vehicles that never seem to last long on the back-country roads.

On one of my visits, Junior was excited. "Boy, I'm glad you come by today," he began. "I traded a carving for that little piece o' land over there, got a 'bull-noser' to clean it off, and they're comin' tonight with a brand new mobile home. And then they're goin' to drill me a well right over there...." He talked on, but I only absorbed part of what he said. A new benefactor was supplying Junior with a 70-foot mobile home and the new well, in exchange for carvings and for work refinishing antiques.

Of course, I was glad that he and his family were getting a better home, and there was no question that a proper water supply was needed by the large and growing family. But I kept thinking of what he was giving up. For Junior enjoyed in full measure what I had returned from the city to catch a taste of: independence; closeness to nature; a simple way of life. How much of this was he trading away? And how long could a sensitive artist be happy refinishing antiques? Knowing Junior's nature, I had the thought that it just wouldn't work.

Evidently it didn't. I don't know what happened to the agreement, but last time I stopped at Junior's, the mobile home was gone and the family was back in the shanty. They did have the new well, though, I was glad to see.

Still, I realized more than ever that my Ozarks are changing.

*M*any other "last-of-a-kind" characters are scattered through the Ozarks. One is Hobart Owen. A lifelong peddler who has hauled his wares over the hills by horse and wagon and pickup truck, he is now confined by poor health to a store building in Forsyth, Missouri. Hobart deals in feed, seed, fertilizer, salt, motor oil, fresh eggs, soda pop, and about anything else that he can get hauled in and dispense at a small profit. He writes up sales tickets with a flourish, but seldom moves from his couch, and customers make their own change from an open cash register.

Another is Fred Dirst, still dwelling on the banks of the Buffalo River at the deserted mining town of Rush, Arkansas, where he first came in the boom year of 1915. If a visitor appears genuinely interested, Dirst will conduct a tour of some of the old mines, vividly describing what it was like when zinc ore was being extracted. But mostly he sits in a chair at the mouth of Rush Creek or at his mobile home back in the trees, collecting a few modest fees for camping, boat launching, and canoe and boat rentals.

In 1953, Dirst acquired more than 300 acres along the Buffalo at Rush Creek. Ever since, he has resisted the temptation to sell off an acre or two at a time to vacation-home builders. Soon his land will pass to the National Park Service under an act of Congress designating the Buffalo as a national river; but the law provides for an occupant's option that could permit Fred to live out his life on the land. Those who know Fred can't imagine his moving anywhere else.

And Uncle Aaron Stevens, at 88 the last surviving blacksmith in Stone County, Arkansas, is pretty sure to live out his days on Roasting Ear Creek in sight of most of the major occurrences of his life.

"I was born about three mile right across the hill yonder," he said. "My daddy moved when I was two, then moved up here when I was four year old. I been on this place 84 year."

Like most people who have inhabited the Ozark back country, Uncle Aaron did a variety of work to make a living, and like all who have the honorary title of "Uncle," he earned the respect of his neighbors. He lives with his son Ulis and family on the old home place. He still has his blacksmith tools, but seldom uses them now. "I even got too lazy to grow my own tobacco," he says while cutting a store-bought plug.

Most Ozarkians, of course, have adapted to a modern world, but many still find their greatest satisfactions in their ties to simple mountain life.

I first got to know Ralph Gideon several Novembers ago when his son Gene invited me to join in a deer hunt at The Ranch, a rugged hill farm near Cedarcreek, Missouri. Both Gene and I had to work the day before the season opened, so by the time we found the faint lane leading back through the woods it was after six o'clock. Ralph and his friend Harrison Holland were supposed to be on the scene already, but when we pulled up in the yard the old house was dark. We crossed the creaking porch and knocked.

After a minute or so the door opened a few inches, and a voice said, "Well, I'll be dogged! We'd give you guys up and went to bed." The drawl belonged to Ralph, a lean, erect man then about 65.

He lit a kerosene lamp, and as we brought in our things he poked up the fire in the wood stove to heat the supper leftovers. Harrison, who was hard of hearing, snored right through our arrival.

Promptly at 3:30 a.m. there was a clattering at the stove, and I awoke to see Harrison—wide awake now, and clad in long underwear—building a fire in the cook stove. After a breakfast of bacon, eggs, and biscuits with sorghum molasses, we were ready for the other hunters who were joining our party, and Ralph assigned each a station to reduce the possibility of accidents.

My post afforded nary a shot that first

Feather for luck decorates a three-string mountain dulcimer of walnut, made in three days by Judy Klemmedson and Dude Black. Lynn McSpadden fashioned the four-string spruce instrument at left. Relatively simple to play, folk dulcimers can sound hauntingly melancholy.

morning, and at noon I hiked back to the house for lunch and coffee. Ralph sensed my disappointment. "Get up in the stand in that cedar tree, and I'll send you a deer," he said.

I didn't put much stock in that, but I did as I was told. It was cold and damp that afternoon, and I evidently stayed too long in one position on the narrow planks —for when a twig broke below and behind me, I suddenly realized I was numb all over. Forcing my neck to turn, I looked over my shoulder. Just emerging from the brush was a large doe—legal quarry at this season. She stopped in the clearing, not 15 feet away, while I strained to coax my unresponsive legs into a shooting position. The gun was like lead. I picked up the rhythm of the animal's condensed breath, and realized it was keeping perfect cadence with my own. Suddenly, the doe looked up at my contorted body, studied me for a moment, then wheeled and disappeared.

Back at the house that evening, Ralph asked me with a twinkle whether I'd seen anything. I sheepishly admitted what had happened, realizing then that he had been quite serious about driving a deer in my direction. Knowing the animals' trails, tracks, and sounds, he had sent one unerringly to the clearing under my perch. My embarrassment was quelled, fortunately, by fried ham, pinto beans, cornbread, and "sock-eye gravy" made with ham drippings and coffee.

After that weekend I began to visit with Ralph often, and never failed to come away with some gem of folklore.

Ralph was retired when I met him, but he still kept a large garden, and took on a few cabinet-building jobs in his workshop, including some for me. I found that when he works he is a perfectionist, wastes practically nothing, and can create much from the leftovers of others.

In the last three years Ralph has suffered two severe heart attacks. But he has returned each time to the little farmstead near Forsyth where he and his wife, Clara, reared six children on his wages as a mechanic and carpenter and the yield from their ten acres. He seems even more attuned to wildlife now than on

that day he sent me a deer. One morning recently he pointed out more than two dozen nesting birds, including a wily mockingbird that fetches Ralph with urgent cries every time a snake menaces her nest. The field beyond the garden is primarily a preserve now, inhabited by several coveys of quail and visited by an occasional deer.

People who have lived in the mountains know that life there is not easy, and as I came to know Ralph I learned something of the price he and Clara had paid to live in the Ozarks. He told me about growing up on a farm in Christian County, Missouri, and about rearing a large family during the Great Depression—a story I understood, for I spent my childhood on a hill farm in that same period.

Troubles cascaded on the Gideons. In 1935 Joella, then a first-grader, fell ill with blood poisoning, and Ralph and Clara tended her around the clock for a week. In 1938 Chloris, the oldest child and a high school junior, died of meningitis. Then on a beautiful February morning in 1941, the rented house burned with virtually all the family's possessions.

The children and Clara were scattered to the homes of relatives, while Ralph stayed on the place—"My daddy always told me, 'You've got to find something where you lost it,'" he recalled.

"I was walkin' through that field yonder when it came to me what I had to do. I decided that somehow I was goin' to build a house on my rocky old ten acres and get my family back together again."

At Round Mountain, near Goodnight Hollow, Ralph found Uncle Charley Ingenthron sitting on a pile of lumber which had been sawed for him on shares.

"What do you need?" asked Uncle Charley. Replied Ralph, "I need a bill of oak lumber and a bunch of them split rocks. I ain't got the money, and I may never have."

He got his materials, and soon he had the walls of a new house standing.

"It's beautiful," conceded Clara, "but how're you going to get a roof over it?"

Ralph went to see Arch Mayden at the bank in Branson and borrowed $125. He bought the roofing, outside decking, doors, windows, and screens for $121 — leaving $4 to spare.

The house was still only a shell, with rough subfloors and bare two-by-fours where room walls would be, but Ralph set out to gather up his family.

He had done most of the work himself, and it would take him several more years to finish and furnish the house. But neighbors and friends helped in remarkable and heartening ways. Hobart Owen loaned a truck. A lad Ralph had regarded as something of a hellion dug tirelessly at the new cellar. Sometimes people drove up in passenger cars and from the trunks unloaded stones and building materials; others donated furniture.

At one point Ralph went to California, got a good-paying job, and saved enough to pay off the money he owed. Once that was done, he turned down a promotion and came home; he was eager to return to his ten acres, and content to work as a carpenter on whatever jobs he could find nearby.

Ralph and his family fondly recall those days in the unfinished house with curtained-off rooms. And all six of the children still live in the Ozarks.

Jobs are not nearly so scarce in the Ozarks these days, what with tourism growing, an influx of retirees, and the locating of numerous industrial plants in the region. Even so, if one picks precisely the place he wants to live, he may not find employment right at hand.

When Lowell Myers came to work in the Springfield, Missouri, printing plant where the magazine I edit is produced, I quickly learned he was not an ordinary man. He was not only a skilled operator of typesetting equipment but also the author of an article we were about to publish. Although he had only a high school education, he was a scholar of Ozark history, of nature, and of the Bible. And he was unusual in another way: He drove a 112-mile round trip each day to reach his job from the place he called Oleo Acres ("one of your cheaper spreads") near Humansville, Missouri.

On the pretense of visiting an old water mill near Oleo Acres, I asked Lowell if

Low hills and deep hollows of the Ozark Plateau and adjacent ranges encompass much of Missouri and Arkansas. Settled during the 19th century largely by hillsmen migrating from the Appalachians, this region of abundant streams increasingly attracts tourists and light industry.

I could ride home with him one Wednesday evening, spend the night, and come back as he returned to work next day.

For the first 50 miles northwest from Springfield the road runs fairly straight through land more reminiscent of prairie than of the irregular hills and valleys of the Ozarks. Then we turned onto a gravel road, crossed a stream, and started up a steep, winding grade. The trees closed in around us, the road got narrower, the houses more infrequent. Lowell pointed out spots where he had seen wild turkey and deer, and I began to get an inkling of why he was willing to invest more than 25,000 miles of driving and 750 hours of travel time a year to live in these hills.

Lowell had described his place as a rough, six-acre site he had purchased and cleared just three years earlier. I was promised a place to sleep in the shed.

Actually Oleo Acres turned out to be a neat, well-kept oasis in the back country. Four-year-old Vance rushed out to greet his daddy while Lowell's wife, Beverly, welcomed him from the door. I could smell the aroma of the supper she was preparing: fried chicken, home-grown vegetables, fresh-baked pie.

Lowell romped with his son while I got a look at what my host considered primitive: a used mobile home; a sturdy red barn for the two horses I saw grazing in the meadow; a trim lawn and flourishing garden; a kennel for bird dogs; and the "shed," which was indeed a storage building but also housed Lowell's study and a comfortable guest room.

How, I wondered, can a man devote so much of his time to driving back and forth to work, keep up such demanding avocations as hunting, fishing, hiking, canoeing, horseback riding, reading, and writing, and still carve a comfortable homestead out of the brush in just a couple of years—and then I decided the secret must lie in part in consuming prodigious quantities of food. Lowell loves to eat, and apparently his city-bred wife loves to cook. As grace was said I realized I was extraordinarily hungry, but I proved no match for my host.

After supper we drove up the valley, which I learned is mostly owned or in-habited by other members of Lowell's family. We mapped out the old foundations and stonework of the pioneer mill site, then headed home.

At Blackjack, Lowell pointed out the Church of God and paused to look over the parking lot, explaining, "I just wanted to see if Beverly and Vancey are still at prayer meetin'. They are, so we'll beat them home."

I realized then that I had invited myself to Lowell's home on an evening when he normally would attend church —and that the family had said nothing, in order to keep me from feeling like an intruder. I apologized, but Lowell quickly dismissed the matter.

Beverly and Vance got home shortly after we did, and we enjoyed ice cream, coffee, and conversation until—mindful of the early hour that we must arise to return to Springfield—I excused myself.

In the shed I opened a window to catch the breeze, and prepared to let the night sounds of Oleo Acres lull me to sleep. Gradually I became aware of a voice, firm but distant. I could hear just clearly enough to know that Lowell was reading aloud from the Bible. After a while the voice was joined by another, and the words became indistinguishable. But their direction was not. Lowell had not missed Wednesday prayer meeting; he had simply postponed it until later in the evening.

Generalizations about Ozark religion are fairly common and often over-simplified. Certainly the Ozarks do not determine the nature of one's religion; but it is my observation that beliefs do tend to intensify in this setting.

As manager of my son's baseball team, I was called one weekend by the sponsors of our Sunday afternoon opponents who asked that the game be postponed a couple of hours so their players could attend a baptismal service. I agreed, and upon learning that it was to be held in Beaver Creek, on the Vesta Floyd farm near Bradleyville, Missouri, I decided to attend myself.

At the barnyard gate I saw a friend, Burl Maggard, who assured me I would be welcome. As I started down the path, I heard a familiar chorus:

Yes, we'll gather at the river,
The beautiful, the beautiful river . . .

Close to a hundred people had gathered on the bank of the clear-flowing stream, dense with midsummer foliage. A bush of pale pink wild roses on the opposite bank formed a backdrop as the Reverend Glesco Roberts explained the significance of what was about to take place. Fully clothed, he strode toward the middle of the stream to explore the path by which he would lead the ten baptismal candidates. Then all joined hands and walked out into the water.

Mr. Roberts is pastor of several small congregations in the vicinity; most of this day's candidates were from the Union Flat General Baptist Church. They ranged in age from about 12 to well past 70. Like the relatives and friends who looked on attentively, they were plainly clad—mostly print dresses for the women, sport shirts and cotton pants for the men, here and there a pair of freshly laundered bib overalls.

It was a simple service: a short passage of Scripture, another hymn, and a brief prayer by the pastor before he carefully bent each candidate backward in turn, immersing each one for a moment in the waters of Beaver Creek.

Some came up spluttering, some laughing, some crying, but in a few minutes they waded drenched and radiant back into the midst of those waiting on the bank. Someone began singing "Amazing Grace," and as the sweet melody gathered strength and I looked at the faces of the singers, it seemed clear to me why religious traditions have changed little in the Ozarks since the first settlers.

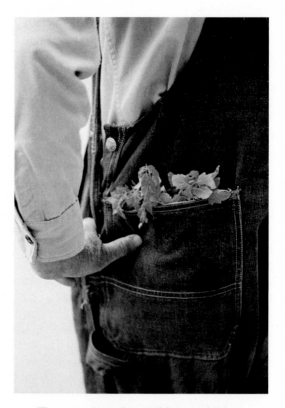

Tomato plant donated by a neighbor nestles in the hip pocket of a Yellville, Arkansas, farmer. Most rural Ozark families maintain gardens, and share plants, cuttings, and then the bounty at harvest time.

*O*ther traditions that have withstood time to remain vital elements of Ozark life are the region's arts and crafts and its folk music. Far from dying out, interest and participation in these have soared in recent years, and have been major cultural aspects of the growing importance of tourism to the Ozark economy.

The early settlers made their tools, housewares, toys, and musical instruments from whatever was available. Now many of the same skills have been revived and refined to provide or supplement the income of Ozark people today.

The interest in old-fashioned skills pursued by Rex Harral, a lean hillsman who lives near Wilburn, Arkansas, goes well beyond what will earn him a dollar. He keeps handy at a surprising number of once-familiar techniques, including some — such as rail splitting, railroad-tie hacking, and plow-point sharpening — that have few commercial possibilities nowadays. He also makes many decorative and useful articles of wood and metal. Every time I see him, he seems to have sharpened up on some obscure craft — tanning leather, perhaps, or making a corncob pipe.

There are literally thousands of participants in the reinvigorated Ozark craft movement, and their wares are displayed at shops, fairs, festivals, and museums throughout the region. Three of the most important and influential contributors to the success of this revival have been the Ozark Arts and Crafts Fair, which takes place each October at the remote crossroads of War Eagle, Arkansas; the region's largest commercial tourist attraction, Silver Dollar City, near Branson, Missouri; and the Ozark Foothills Handicraft Guild.

The War Eagle fair began in 1953 as an exhibit by a small group of weavers. It takes place in an unlikely but charming spot some 20 miles back in the hills from the towns of Rogers, Springdale, Huntsville, and Eureka Springs. A millpond that has outlasted its original use, a quiet river valley, and a house whose pine logs were cut in the 1830's contribute to the atmosphere.

Mrs. Blanche Elliott, the unpaid director, has developed the three-day event into a major show of the region's best art and craft work, with more than 300 exhibitors and an estimated 70,000 visitors each year. The sponsoring organization also conducts seminars to encourage the practice and to improve the quality of traditional craft skills.

Silver Dollar City, by contrast, is a wholly commercial enterprise that has grown up atop Marvel Cave. The cave has been open to visitors since 1894, but not until 1960, with construction of a village of old-style craft shops, did the spot become one of the most popular tourist attractions in the Midwest. Recently Silver Dollar City has increased emphasis on its 1880's theme park aspects, but it remains an extremely important market for the goods and talents of Ozark people. It was from here that Peter Engler gained his reputation as a wood-carver and provided encouragement for the scores of other carvers who now work, and compete, with him.

The Ozark Foothills Handicraft Guild began in the early 1960's as a cooperative sales and promotion venture of craftsmen in north-central Arkansas. The guild operates shops at various highway locations. Leo Rainey of Batesville, a University of Arkansas Cooperative Extension area agent, has assisted the guild since its formation.

One thing that saved the guild from obscurity, possibly from extinction, was the idea of staging a folk festival in 1963 at Mountain View, seat of Stone County, a crucible in which the historic culture of the region still flickered.

To be their headliner, guild leaders turned to a Stone County native and former country schoolteacher: James Morris. As Jimmy Driftwood — a name his grandmother gave him when he was a baby — he had become a popular performer with the Grand Ole Opry in Nashville, Tennessee, with scores of published and recorded songs to his credit, including "The Battle of New Orleans."

Jimmy advised against assembling a country music show with professional stars, and proposed instead an "Arkansas Folk Festival" with local people singing the songs and playing the instruments of their forefathers. The initial enthusiasm for this idea could be gauged by the fact that exactly six persons turned out for the first planning session. But the committee persisted, and soon formed the Rackensack Folklore Society. Rehearsals took place in the Stone County

Courthouse—starting something that hasn't stopped yet.

The 1963 festival was a great success, bringing to the town many times its population, then less than a thousand. The next week a friend asked Jimmy Driftwood, "Are you comin' down to the courthouse Friday night?" Surprised, Jimmy answered, "The festival's over. So are the rehearsals."

"Hell, we ain't ever lettin' that die," came the response.

So began a regular Friday night program of free Rackensack music—on the courthouse lawn when the weather is fine, in the courtroom when it's not—that has continued for more than ten years. Another folklore society performs on Saturday nights, with somewhat less stringent rules regarding instruments and music played. And people hold uncounted numbers of musicals in their homes, or just about any place they can gather with guitar, banjo, fiddle, mandolin, dulcimer, and harmonica.

All through the next decade Mountain View's music festival and the companion craft show grew, until in 1972 it seemed that every conceivable facility in town had been stretched beyond capacity. But by then a new Folk Cultural Center was under construction, scheduled to be finished for the 1973 festival.

Jimmy Driftwood foresees nightly programs of folk music in the new auditorium during the tourist season, a schedule that would offer a more comprehensive range of musicians and talents than has been possible in the once-a-week programs. He mentioned, for example, Seth Mize, whom I remember as a wiry little fiddler who occasionally breaks into a jig while playing. "Nobody knows that Seth can also play the guitar," Jimmy said, "that he can sing, and that although he's semi-illiterate he's composed a lot of songs."

Jimmy insists the new facilities won't change the basic character of the community's musicals. Not everyone agrees.

I discussed these things with Jimmy and his wife, Cleda, in the farmhouse where they have lived since long before he achieved his prominence in the field

Roots of a ginseng plant dangle from the hand of Bobby Blair, an experienced hunter of " 'seng" in the Arkansas woods. An ingredient of soothing ointments and a valuable export to Asia, ginseng has brought him as much as $45 a pound.

of country music. Jimmy gave up that lucrative career several years ago and devotes his time to caring for his land and cattle, heading the Arkansas Parks and Tourism Commission, teaching folklore courses, and furthering the activities of the Rackensack Society. His farm, 12 miles west of Mountain View at the village of Timbo, is in a broad valley lined by steep ridges.

As dusk approached, Cleda carried a cake to the car and we drove south over the ridge to the little town of Fox, where a Saturday night musical in one of the homes has been the custom for more than 15 years. On this occasion the gathering was at the home of Lonnie Lee.

The Lee place is a couple of miles off the highway on a gravel road. As in the house we had just left and so many others in the Ozarks, the kitchen, dining, and living areas were combined in one large room. The walls were decorated with pictures of Lonnie and Nita's nine children, a mounted elk head, a gun rack, and a poster for a country music concert.

Some three dozen people were already assembled, including Seth Mize, Bookmiller Shannon, and other Rackensack members. Outside, laughing children played in the deepening dusk.

The music started at once and went on until after midnight, the congenial group listening, enjoying, sharing, some taking turns singing or playing, others stepping out into the cool night air to talk awhile with the pervasive melody and rhythm as background.

Old English ballads are heard often in the Ozarks, and were that night, but several songs had a distinctive Irish quality —especially those sung and played by Bobby Blair, a dark, lean, 41-year-old fiddler, guitarist, and mandolin player, and his eldest son, Wes, a strapping high school football player as well as a musician. I listened, completely absorbed, to the plaintive "Nola Shannon," "The Sweet Forget-Me-Not," "Burgundy Wine," and "Memory's Lane."

Bobby doesn't pretend to know the origin of these songs. He does know that his family was of Irish descent and came to the Ozarks around 1850 from Tennes-

see. Bobby's father, four uncles, and an aunt were musicians, and the songs they knew were passed on to Bobby, and lately to Wes, in the traditional way.

I asked Bobby to sing "Memory's Lane," a favorite of mine, once more. When he came to the chorus, I suddenly heard another voice from across the room: Lonnie Lee was adding a falsetto counter-melody, an intricate and captivating sound born of dozens of sessions like this one.

Bobby Blair, I came to know, has some reservations about the new Folk Cultural Center; he is dubious that the music played in Stone County homes, on the back stoops, and at the creaky old courthouse will endure and thrive in the cavernous auditorium on the hill.

Eppes Mabry, son of a pioneer stave mill operator, has similar doubts about the future of crafts at the center. Eppes was a carpenter who developed a new vocation by prowling the woods looking for discarded and overlooked logs, stumps, limbs, and knots. Eventually he filled an old chicken house with beautifully grained and burled pieces of black walnut, wild cherry, persimmon, bois d'arc, sassafras, and other woods. Working mainly with a lathe, and under the inspiration he drew from the individuality of the natural forms, Eppes began producing remarkable objects of art.

It was not long until demand for his products outgrew the limits set by time and health. But hope for transforming that accumulated supply of beautiful wood into decorative objects lies in another high school student: Jay Mabry, youngest of Eppes's six children and his only son.

*I*n late summer for many years, Eppes Mabry and Bobby Blair have devoted their weekends to hunting ginseng. Ozark people have been digging the roots of this elusive plant since sometime in the 19th century. As to its use, few have more than a vague notion—other than that they can sell all they can find to pharmaceutical manufacturers. The price of ginseng has consistently stayed well above $30 a pound in recent years.

Folk medicine has a firm foothold in the Ozarks, and many people still use preparations made from golden seal, bloodroot, mullein, slippery elm, wahoo, witch hazel, and mayapple. But I have heard of only one instance in which ginseng was incorporated in a home remedy. Perhaps the frugal people of these hills never really considered using something so readily convertible to cash, particularly when the woods were full of other medicinal plants which had little or no market value.

"'Seng hunters" traditionally have been a secretive lot, jealous of their knowledge, techniques, and hunting grounds. I learned why after Eppes and Bobby invited me to go with them on a warm September day.

We wore cotton clothing and leather boots and carried walking sticks. Eppes and Bobby each had a small mattock and a canvas sack.

The only unusual portions of our outfits were the leggings: sections of inner tubes cut in lengths to reach from ankles to hips, slipped on over the feet, and wired at top to the belt. No matter how you wear these rubber parentheses, the effect is comical: If the curve of the tube is toward the front, you look as if you are crouching, ready to leap; with the curves turned to the sides, the effect is a caricature of a bow-legged cowboy. Nevertheless, when Bobby showed me the drying skins of three timber rattlers he had killed on successive days, I willingly put on the hot, awkward tubes.

Ginseng grows slowly, so an active hunter must wait years to return to a previously productive site; in the meantime he searches out new ones. Eppes and Bobby decided to try the vicinity of Roasting Ear Creek, and we stopped to ask Uncle Aaron Stevens for clues.

The weathered old gentleman was peeling a washtub of apples. He gladly offered what help he could.

"I was comin' off that ridge yonder," he recalled. "Been huntin' some cows that'd strayed back over them hills. I was almost down the hill and headin' for the house when I realized I was in a big patch of 'seng."

Sawmill operator Ernest Blair takes a moment from work near Bradleyville, Missouri. Farmers clearing cedar trees sell the wood to Ernest and his son, Bill. The fragrant cedar ends up as flooring, closet lining, and souvenir boxes.

"How long ago's that been, Old Timer?" inquired Eppes, using the nickname his father had given the blacksmith.

"Four or five year," replied Uncle Aaron. His pale blue eyes peered from beneath the battered felt hat at the hills he has seen nearly every day of his life. "I ain't been able to get out much since, and I just don't know if it's still there or not."

The old man had described a lower part of a northeast slope, heavily shaded—a prime prospect for ginseng. We drove as close as we could, then set out on foot. The slapping of our inner-tube leggings gave me the thought that they should be as effective in warning snakes away from our path as in repelling their fangs.

When we got close to the base of the ridge we broke file, and Eppes and Bobby began working slowly upgrade through the dense brush, examining—it seemed to me as I floundered between them—every plant in the woods.

Little sunlight came through the dense cover of mixed hardwoods. I could sense that the hunters felt they were close to a find. "Here's the pointer," called Bobby, showing me a pretty little fern. Moments later the hunters discovered another fern found frequently with ginseng—and then we were standing right in the middle of the spot Uncle Aaron had described.

But now there was only a series of empty holes, as if someone had turned up random spadefuls of dirt over an area 20 yards square. The patch had been thoroughly dug. Eppes and Bobby examined the evidence. Eppes frowned and rolled his blue eyes, and Bobby clucked disgustedly. Apparently the rival 'seng hunter had beaten them to the patch by several months. There was not a single living ginseng plant to be seen.

Bobby began working up the slope while Eppes circled around into the draw. Fortunately, no 'seng hunter ever seems to find all the plants. Soon Bobby called out that he had discovered one at the base of a large tree.

My first look at the leaves, grouped in clusters of five, surprised me; they were much like those of several other woodland plants. But I soon learned what was distinctive about ginseng, and also about the way in which a thoughtful mountain man harvests it.

Bobby stood motionless, studying the ground all around his feet. He was surveying the mature plants that he would dig, and also the tiny seedlings surrounding them, which he would leave. As he gently examined each plant, I began to detect some of the distinguishing characteristics. Some sprays of leaves had turned a brilliant gold. Under those leaves were small red berries containing the precious seeds for future plants.

His examination completed, he dropped to his knees and with deft strokes of his mattock loosened the matting of leaves and soil around the plant. Then he lifted the roots out intact.

While one could easily mistake the leaves, the roots of ginseng are unique. Tuberous, knobby, often developing grotesque shapes, they are topped by the crowns of previous years' growth stacked one above another.

Eppes and Bobby made several other scattered finds that day, depositing the roots carefully in the sacks they carried. Also into the sacks went most of the seeds, but some were planted right where they were found. Here and there growing plants were intentionally passed by, left to seed a promising area for future years.

Some success has been achieved in growing ginseng in garden plots; but Eppes and Bobby deposit their seeds in likely locations in the wild, accepting the risk that other hunters will harvest from their sowing. The domestic variety is judged less valuable than ginseng from the woods, but that is not my friends' reason for sowing their seeds there. They simply feel a responsibility to aid nature in the survival of this strange plant.

I thought again of the fragile music Bobby Blair sings, and of the unusual art form that has evolved from Eppes Mabry's imagination and background. Will these men and their people, their talents and their values, continue to flourish in these quiet mountains?

My optimism grows when I remember the sensitive 'seng hunter pressing seeds into the ground and nurturing the fledgling plants.

Seven hillsmen, humorously but carefully detailed from wood, stand on a split rail.

The carver's art

PUTTING KNIFE BLADE to wood seems to come naturally to mountain folk. Some simply whittle shavings off one stick after another while thinking, talking, listening, or whistling. Others carry carving to a fine art, and some make a living at it.

Style and subject matter vary widely among artists. Jim Maxwell of Branson, Missouri, who created the figures above, likes to stick to caricatures. Ivan Denton of Mountainburg, Arkansas, is intrigued by wildlife and western scenes. Versatile Junior Cobb, who lives near Three Brothers, Arkansas, can produce life-size human figures with the same accuracy that he brings to shaping tiny animals.

The prices such carvers ask depend upon a work's size and complexity; some bring hundreds of dollars. Cobb, who has been carving since childhood, seems to produce only in proportion to his immediate need for money. Denton took up the craft 20 years ago, after breaking off a walnut limb to prop up a sagging fence. "I noticed the wood's deep reddish brown color," he said. "Later I went back and cut off whole blocks of it and carved horses from them." The serious, hardworking Denton likes to quote a couplet he attributes to another wood-carver:

To keep the wolf from the door,
Howl less and whittle more.

Limbering up the slingshot he calls his
"beanflip," Junior Cobb takes one of his
frequent breaks from "whittlin'." Junior,
his wife, Helen, and their five children
live in a shanty next to the rustic workshop
(below) where he transforms mountain woods
into his highly popular carvings. As do
many sculptors, he usually works with
models clearly in mind. The 16-inch-high
hillbillies opposite resemble neighbors.

Both his art and his life-style reflect Ivan Denton's interest in western subjects. He walks this woodland trail often to feed the ten horses he keeps on his 400 acres. "I like to go for a walk or get on a horse knowing that ten minutes after I leave, I can't be found or contacted," he says. He tries to move silently, observing the animals and birds: "If you get quiet, it's amazing how little you disturb nature as you ride along." What he sees finds expression in elements of scenes such as that of the mare and foal under attack, opposite. He, too, carves faces familiar to him; the cowboy's features mirror his own.

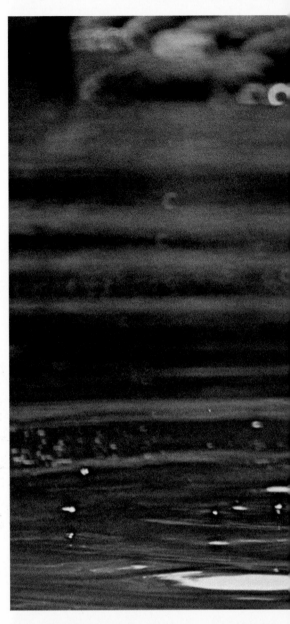

Terry Denton, eldest of Ivan's four daughters, cools off in a creek on the family property. Terry began carving nine years ago; at 23 she has earned recognition as one of the Ozarks' outstanding young artists. The girl with the bucket and the seated lass strumming the mandolin exemplify her mastery of fine detail; both figures measure about six inches high. One of her tiny horses prances saucily on a finger. Terry and her father sometimes collaborate on larger sculptures. Her sisters Janet, 20, and Laura, 16, also carve.

4

The Rockies: "We can do anything we have to"

by Zeke Scher

HARDSCRABBLE CANYON and Hoza Flats both help to conceal the Wet Mountain Valley to the very last moment. The first time I drove that road, up from the Arkansas River near Florence, Colorado, through foothills with an occasional eroded ridge popping out above the piñons, scrub oak, and ponderosa pine, I didn't expect much. I figured that if southern Colorado's Custer County were something to see, someone would have told me about it long before now.

A main trail of the mountain-dwelling Ute Indians went this way. As late as 1861 the Utes fought the Arapahoes here. The trail led west to the Utes' summer campground, the 8,000-foot-high valley that now was my destination.

Not much has been written about this remote portion of the Rocky Mountains' eastern slope since Lt. Zebulon Pike struggled through the snows of the valley in January 1807. His journal tells how he spent two weeks just trying to find a way out. Before he found Medano Pass to the San Luis Valley on the other side, he had left three men behind with frozen feet.

But now it was a warm June day after the mildest of winters. As I dipped down from Hoza Flats, the waiting surprise was suddenly revealed: a valley 10 miles wide and 40 miles long, its backdrop an incredible panorama of the Sangre de Cristo Mountains, a line of bold, pyramidal peaks rising to more than 14,000 feet against the western sky.

It's no wonder, I thought, that Ben Kettle's family has spent a century here.

Young Will Kettle and his bride, Isabella, arriving from faraway England, must have been as awed as I with those Sangre de Cristos when they drove a covered wagon into the valley in July 1872. Six months later, Will made up his mind to become a United States citizen, and on New Year's Day of 1873—having sold his team and wagon to buy supplies the previous fall—he started walking the 30 miles northeast through the Wet Mountains to Cañon City, seat of Colorado Territory's Fremont County. Caught midway in a snowstorm, he found shelter at a ranch, and finally made it to Cañon City on January 4. At the courthouse he declared his intention to renounce allegiance to Queen Victoria. The signed document is a family heirloom.

Then he walked back home.

A hundred years later his grandson, Ben, lives in the house Will built of hand-hewn red spruce logs dragged down from the mountainside. There have been changes and additions, but the original cabin forms the core of the house.

Will raised hay for mules used in the mines at nearby Rosita and Silver Cliff during the boom years of the 1870's and '80's. Little by little he acquired a herd of cattle, turning to pure-bred Herefords in 1916.

He insisted that his three daughters and one son obtain the education he never had; he sent them all off to college and graduate studies, and his encouragement and their effort produced a professor, a school superintendent, and a poet among his daughters, and a teacher and civil engineer in his son, Charles.

The son returned to the ranch after he married, and joined Will in the growing cattle operation. But the Depression of the 1930's brought the partners severe financial problems, made worse by a series of dry years that failed to produce sufficient feed to supply the livestock through the winter. One day Will and Charles listed the 6,000 acres with a Colorado Springs real estate agent.

"That really shocked me," Ben said. He was 18 and ready for college when his father and grandfather decided to sell. "As a boy I hadn't assumed responsibility to the degree Dad expected, and I guess I didn't show much interest in the ranch; but the interest was actually there all the time, and I realized it when he put the place up for sale.

"I asked him to take the ranch off the listing, because I wanted to make it my career—as he and Grandpa Will had done. He agreed to hold on, but only if I

(Continued on page 138)

Roughhewn planks frame 80-year-old Jennie Schmid in the front doorway of her home on Wilson Mesa in southwestern Colorado. She has lived on the mesa for 73 years, although she now spends the harsh Rocky Mountain winters in the town of Colona. "Three generations of my family have ranched right around here," she says with pride.

Darkening clouds build toward an afternoon storm above Wilson Mesa, a rolling Colorado

plateau touched by gold in October. A twisting road links the mesa's four ranches.

Raindrops from an autumn shower course the living room window of Loey Ringquist, owner of the Faraway Ranch on Wilson Mesa. Cradling one of her eight dogs in her lap, Loey rides through a stand of golden aspens on her 1,500 acres. She spends many hours exploring the mountains, looking for abandoned cabins and mines and collecting curiosities—old bottles, trinkets, tools, barbed wire. At present only animals—including a llama named Tina—share the ranch with her, but she plans to build a home for underprivileged children. "It's so beautiful, I want more than the cows and sheep to see it; living here might influence some youngsters' lives for the good," she says. "The only way to answer to yourself is to do something for others."

Wearing a glass-cutter's apron of heavy leather, owner Bob Dietz stands in the aisle of the century-old Jenkins McKay Hardware Company in Black Hawk, Colorado. His daughter, Shawnie, 2, peers from between his legs. Bob's wife, Sharen (left, above), helps him manage the store, which retains much of its character of early mining days. The Dietzes' stock ranges from mousetraps to power tools, and includes kerosene chandeliers and the placer mining pans stacked on the floor. Miners established Black Hawk in 1859 after the discovery of gold in nearby gulches; within a dozen years the cluster of shacks had become a bustling town with schools, courts, and a municipal government. Today Black Hawk's population totals only about 200, and the town stays considerably quieter than when the façade of the welding shop at left acquired its imposing advertisement.

would take veterinary medicine in college so I'd have a vocation to fall back on if I got tired of the ranch."

Will, of course, was delighted with the agreement. Ben had enrolled in an accelerated course at Colorado State College of Agriculture and Mechanic Arts when the hardy pioneer died in his sleep on Christmas Eve of 1941 at the age of 92. In 1944 Ben came back to the Wet Mountain Valley as Doc Kettle.

On the June morning on which I arrived at the ranch, nearly three decades later, the Kettle household was bustling. It was time to pick out the "heavies"—the cows expected to calve during the next week—and move them into the home pasture.

There are more than a thousand head of cattle on the San Isabel Ranch—named for the adjoining national forest—but Ben manages the operation with only two men on the payroll. That means everybody in the family helps out, especially when it comes to cutting out the heavies each week of the calving period, from May to August.

Ben's parents still take an active interest in the ranch, I learned, and often visit from their home in Littleton, Colorado, where they retired in 1960.

"You want to ride?" Ben asked, holding White Raisin, a Quarter Horse mare, for me. Ben's wife, Elizabeth—or Bet—and their daughters, Dianna, 19, and Bonnie, 12, saddled up too. We moved the herd into one corner of the meadow.

Riding a bay Quarter Horse stallion named Five-or-Nine, Ben looked over the white-faced Herefords. One at a time the cows he and foreman Boyd Moon designated were cut out of the herd and driven across the road to the pasture where their calves would be born.

Ben is as determined to develop a perfect beef animal as Grandpa Will was to establish himself in these mountains in the first place. Everything that happens to one of the Kettles' registered Herefords—from birth to sale—is recorded. When it comes time for breeding, Ben and Bet carefully select the best bulls for the best cows.

"I enjoy the challenge of genetically improving the seed stock that will end up producing better beef," Ben said. "I guess about all I do enjoy is working on the ranch. It's hard now to see myself doing anything else."

He never really planned to do anything else, although for ten years after college he also practiced veterinary medicine among his neighbors. When that began to take too much time from ranch duties, he dropped his practice.

The Kettle property runs to the base of the massive mountains that rise abruptly from the valley floor. From the cutting pasture it's about five miles—the clear air makes it seem less—to the wooded slopes. As elevation increases, the forest changes from pine to aspen to fir and spruce, and then above the 11,000-foot timberline rise rocky scarps and crags. On the shaded northern faces of the peaks, snow lingers all summer.

Spanish explorers, the story goes, broke camp one morning just as the sun was rising on these mountains. As one of them watched in fascination, the snow-capped heights took on a deep red glow, and he uttered a fervent *"Sangre de Cristo!"*—blood of Christ.

The blood-red phenomenon doesn't happen often, said Ben Kettle, but he has witnessed it numerous times in his 50 years. My mornings on the ranch yielded only views of a glorious golden yellow.

Several times I saw the tall, quiet-spoken rancher standing and looking at the mountains. "They're my friends," he said with conviction. "They offer a tremendous sense of security, of stability. On a ranch you work from one emergency to another, but the mountains are always there. They're one thing I don't have to worry about.

"I know that if the wind comes from the east, they'll catch any moisture and deposit it as rain down here or as snow up there. That's important, because the prevailing winds are from the southwest, and usually dry; their moisture has been dropped off in the San Juans."

Bet, too, talked about the Sangre de Cristos with affection, but sometimes she finds them frightening, especially during a winter storm. Then, she said, the *Viento Blanco*—the White Wind— rips the snow from the peaks and slopes and drives it in great clouds across the land. "At times like that you can't see the mountains, but you feel them. It's hard, when they seem so hostile, to remember how much we owe them. But our whole livelihood depends on them, for without the Sangre de Cristos there's no water, and without water there's no ranching in the Wet Mountain Valley.

"And," she added, "they're so beautiful!"

As much as he loves the mountains, Ben has never had any desire to climb them. Still, he has no doubt he could climb and cross the range if he set his mind to it. "We take a lot of pride in meeting whatever challenges Mother Nature tosses at us— and she can throw some pretty wild curves here," he said. "I think we can do anything we have to."

Technology has removed much of the sense of isolation in the Rockies, no matter how far back or how far up you search. The Kettles, for example, have a one-party telephone; and in a corner of the hundred-year-old log room, across from the original window panes, is a color television console.

Still, Ben worries about the future of the ranch. Three sons—the oldest children—have so far shown no interest in taking over. "I wouldn't force anyone into drudgery; a person should enjoy his work," said Ben. "Maybe one of the girls will marry a boy who's interested."

Each morning when early chores are over, Ben heads for the kitchen to put together his specialty, pancakes and sausage. Bet reclaims the premises to prepare noontime dinner, the day's big meal: some sort of beef (all of the herd aren't prizewinners, she points out). Supper is a

Gold, silver, and lush grazing lands lured the first settlers to the lofty reaches of the Rockies, largest mountain system in North America. Today's new wave of adventurers comprises skiers, hunters, tourists.

light meal. As often as not, neighbors or other friends are present, sitting around the long kitchen table. The Kettle family, right back to Will and Isabella, have always been sociable.

"I remember when I was in grade school studying American history," Ben said, "I asked Grandpa Will to tell me about any Indian troubles he'd had.

"He answered me, 'What Indian troubles? They're people like anyone else. You can get along with them if you try.' He said the Utes would look into the cabin window—that one right there—and he'd invite them in for something to eat."

The dry spring had made the valley look like much of the arid West, stunting the growth of native grass, but Ben's 600 acres of alfalfa and irrigated pasture were doing well with water from the three branches of Taylor Creek that cross the ranch and empty into Grape Creek. Sprinklers about the white, one-story ranch house kept the yard green, and Bet's columbines and Oriental poppies provided splashes of blue, red, yellow, and orange. Beside the road grew a tall Canadian willow tree that came to the ranch in the same covered wagon that brought Will and Isabella Kettle to Colorado Territory. Cottonwoods, cedars, and spruce trees, all planted by Will or his descendants, also cast their shade.

Ben likes to talk about his grandparents, and his parents, and the mountains that inspired them. But most of all he likes to talk about cattle. "I'm not close to my goal yet," he said, his green eyes and tanned face growing animated, "but I think I can do the job better than anyone else. I know I'm going to produce a superior Hereford."

West of the Wet Mountain Valley, you cross the Continental Divide at 11,312-foot Monarch Pass. On a clear day you can glimpse some hundred miles to the southwest the jagged, unsymmetrical San Juan Mountains, one of the nation's wildest ranges. Here on the Rockies' western slope all waters flow eventually to the Pacific Ocean, whereas the San Isabel Ranch's creeks on the eastern slope drain to the Gulf of Mexico.

It is 200 miles on a westward line from the Kettles' place to the 90-mile-long Uncompahgre Plateau, which rises to 10,000 feet west of Montrose, Colorado, and abuts the San Juans on the south, the colorful canyonlands near Grand Junction on the north.

The southern portion of the Uncompahgre (the word is Ute for "place of red waters") is dense forest of pine, Engelmann spruce, Douglas fir, and aspen, broken by canyons, grassy hills, and sage flats. The Forest Service calculates a population of 11,600 mule deer, 575 elk, 115 black bears—and two families of humans, living in a 2,200-acre enclave known as Sanborn Park. The land was homesteaded before 1905, when President Theodore Roosevelt established the Uncompahgre National Forest. Nine adults and eight children live here and earn a livelihood in a manner rarely found any more in the Rockies: dry-land farming, without benefit of irrigation.

The families are the Marolfs and the Irvines. Roy and Sarah Marolf, two of their sons, Everett and Edwin, and the sons' wives and children occupy three adjoining farms. Mrs. Dora Irvine, her son, Doyle, and his wife and children live in two houses on another farm about a mile away.

There are two ways to communicate with the families at Sanborn Park, and both are indirect. One is by addressing mail to a Norwood, Colorado, post office box, a very long 17 miles from Sanborn Park by a narrow dirt road up and down two treacherous hills with numerous switchbacks. The other way is by message relayed by a Norwood short-wave radio operator to the receiver in Doyle Irvine's home.

"We checked into having phone service installed," said Roy Marolf. "The closest company was in Nucla, Colorado —that's about 30 miles away. They said it would cost us $5,000 for five phones to be installed. The real problem was that the only local calls we could make would be to Nucla, and we don't know anyone in Nucla. All other calls would be charged as long distance."

So the Marolfs and Irvines rigged up a

phone system among themselves, using old crank-operated equipment bought from the telephone company, in order to talk to each other and to the school.

The children may not be able to call up many friends, but they find ways to use the phone. I was visiting with Doyle and Janet Irvine when Carol, 10, walked out the door, across the yard 50 feet, and into her grandmother's house. A moment later the phone rang—five times, the Irvines' signal.

"Do you think Grandma would mind if I turned on her TV?" asked Carol from across the yard. Grandma was away.

"No, I don't think she would mind," Janet replied with a smile.

"We don't miss an outside phone because we never had one—and besides, we can call Doyle in an emergency," Roy Marolf told me. "Of course, we haven't had an emergency yet."

In 1967 Doyle Irvine purchased short-wave radio equipment after getting a Forest Service contract to make fire-weather reports from mid-April to the end of October. Every noon he checks the gauges in his weather box and transmits to the ranger station at Norwood the readings for humidity, wind direction, and wind speed, and the precipitation and temperatures during the previous 24 hours. He also serves as a fire warden, watching for and reporting big fires, fighting small ones.

Doyle has never seen the Sanborn Park temperature higher than 88°—the average summer high is 78°—nor lower than 38° below zero. The usual, or "comfortable," winter low is 20° below at his 7,860-foot elevation.

Since his father's death in 1970, Doyle's primary job is running the 400-acre farm. He keeps half of it in wheat and oats, the rest in pasture. His 150 hens supply eggs for about 15 longtime customers in Norwood. He has some Hereford cattle, with which he's assisted by Blue, an Australian shepherd.

Blue and the four saddle horses keep a running skirmish going: They nose at him and he barks and nips at them. But, said their owner, the horses never kick Blue, and Blue never bites them.

Hard-rock miners ride an ore bucket into the Smith Mine near Black Hawk. In the small four-man operation, each must be an engineer, carpenter, mason, and explosives expert. The mine's ore (above) yields gold, silver, copper, zinc, and lead.

Ramshackle remnant of Colorado mining booms of the 1880's, the pump house of the Sheep Mountain Tunnel Mill perches on a rock outcrop above the Crystal River. Powered by the roiling water, the mill once serviced three nearby mines, crushing ore for extraction of silver and other metals. Trees at left screen the ghost town of Crystal City, built in 1880 and deserted by 1920. Abandoned towns dot the slopes of the Rocky Mountains; as mines played out, the workers moved on. Today far fewer people live in rural parts of the Rockies than in either the Appalachians or the Ozarks.

Outside the living room's picture window, as we talked, six mule deer calmly grazed in the grainfield next to the house.

"Living up here, folks sort of depend on one another," Doyle said. "Whoever goes into town checks the mail for the rest, and sometimes we pick up supplies for each other.

"You know, except for new equipment and modernized houses, it's just about the same here as when I was a boy going to Sanborn Park School."

The children carry on various 4-H Club projects—Carol won a blue ribbon for her white bread at the San Miguel County Fair—and the Sanborn Park families enter a float in the Norwood Pioneer Day parade every September. They have won first prize the last five years.

When I had written to notify the Marolfs of my plan to visit Sanborn Park in July, the reply asked me to meet everyone for lunch at the school. Lunchtime could be whenever I arrived. The kids would enjoy the break from class routine.

School? In July?

As it happens, July is right in the middle of the term at Sanborn Park School. Years ago the Montrose School District board decided—because the weather is so bad on the plateau in winter, and the roads are sometimes impassable—that "summer vacation" for the Marolf and Irvine youngsters (the only students in the one-room school) should be January through March, give or take a few weeks—just so they get in 180 school days a year.

The schoolhouse, on Everett Marolf's property, is centrally located: The Marolf youngsters—Jenny, 10, and Nannette, 7 —live to the northeast, the Irvine children to the south. The Irvines—Bruce, 12, and Carol (Darrel is only 4)—have a choice: They can ride their bikes along the road in 15 minutes, or they can follow an old cow trail and make it in half that. Their parents say the kids can walk the trail as fast as they can ride it.

When Bruce Dale and I reached the school for the lunchtime social, Roy Marolf, 72-year-old head of his clan, was waiting for us. He took some good-natured ribbing from the family for being "all slicked up"—shiny brown boots, sharply ironed plaid shirt, and a new pair of jeans. "There are guests, aren't there?" was his response.

Roy took a seat on the steps of the house trailer that serves as the schoolteacher's residence, and accepted a plate of food brought from the colorful table supplied by the women of Sanborn Park: barbecued beef, potato and fruit salads, baked beans and deviled eggs, hot homemade rolls and cinnamon buns, cookies, punch, coffee. The four students, accustomed to a somewhat less extravagant school lunch, tried some of everything— several times.

The little frame schoolhouse had just been painted by the school district's maintenance crew. Color scheme had been left to the painters, and the result was impressive to say the least: sills and posts a brilliant orange; everything else, snow white.

In the school yard, beyond the trailer, were long cultivated rows neatly marked *Jenny, Nannette, Carol,* and *Bruce.* A noble effort was under way for the three-month growing season: corn, peas, beans, radishes, lettuce, carrots, turnips, onions, beets, and potatoes. The children irrigated the rows with a hose connected to a well pump.

I also saw extensive gardens at each home. Everett Marolf's wife, Ella, said she almost never has to buy vegetables—but she was open to any suggestion on how to keep the deer away from her garden.

"In one night they cleaned out a whole row of cabbage," she said. "But that's not as bad as the problem of skunks getting through the fence to the chickens." One year she lost 150 of her 200 chickens.

The Marolfs have tried both lights and noise to scare away the abundant wildlife, but the raids continue.

Ella is an avid reader, accomplished painter, and creative cook. Her willingness to experiment in the kitchen comes in handy in unexpected ways. When Taffy, the white "Pekipoo" dog—half Pekingese, half poodle—had a run-in with a skunk, "I wanted to wash her in tomato juice, because it kills the odor, but I didn't have any on hand," Ella said. "But I had a lot of tomato sauce. So I diluted that and gave Taffy a real good scrubbing. We had a pink pooch for a while—but she didn't smell."

Ella does remarkable things with rhubarb—60 pounds of it plus 60 pounds of sugar, 34 lemons, and "lots of raspberries." After it sits long enough—"nobody can move that vat anyway"—a rhubarb wine results that is stored away for special occasions. "Last winter we had company all through the holidays," Ella recalled. "That was really hard on the rhubarb wine."

All the Marolfs raise Shorthorn cattle and cultivate oats, barley, and wheat. There is no source of irrigation water for their high-plateau fields, and they must depend on the fickle Colorado weather.

Often the moisture comes in the form of dramatic electrical storms. The ruins of Roy's barn lie in the open where it burned in June 1969 after lightning struck. Everett lost five cows that were standing under a tree hit by a lightning bolt. And twice lightning has hit television antennas and burned out the sets. It's no wonder that lightning worries everybody in Sanborn Park more than anything else.

"That's honestly the only thing that scares me up here—the lightning," Ella declared. "All you can do is pull all the plugs and wait—inside," said Everett.

But electrical storms don't provide the only spectacles of western skies. Residents of the Rockies often witness splendid and inspiring sunsets in unimaginable shades of red, orange, yellow, and purple. And against such light are silhouetted grand shapes of the high-country rock formations, resulting in effects beyond the artistry of the boldest and most talented painter. I watched such a sunset as it cast a pink tinge on the San Juan peaks that frame the lower Uncompahgre Plateau, while their long shadows crept across the remarkably flat grainfields of Sanborn Park.

Roy Marolf has spent 45 years on the plateau. He bought 120 acres here in 1927, built a house, invited his childhood

Skull and sweeping horns of a Rocky Mountain bighorn sheep hang in Rachel's saloon in South Park City, a street of restored pioneer buildings at Fairplay, Colorado. A stuffed great horned owl peers from behind the bar. The restoration, a project of Fairplay citizens, has brought together buildings, furnishings, and equipment from throughout Park County.

sweetheart out from eastern Colorado, married her in Montrose, and spent the honeymoon in the new home. Eventually he multiplied his holdings and shared them with his sons.

"We like it here because it's quiet," he said, "and it's a real good climate—kind of rough in the winter, but not too bad. We've spent very little on doctor bills. The kids weren't ever very sick."

Changes in the farm routine haven't been many, and the main innovations are remembered clearly. "I'll never forget February 3, 1955," says Roy. "That was the day we first got electricity. The boys and I put in the poles and lines and did all the interior wiring ourselves."

Sarah continued using the wood-burning kitchen stove until 1964—"It kept the kitchen so nice and warm," she said —but now all the Sanborn Park households have been converted to electric appliances.

Besides running their own farms, Everett and Edwin have another job: The county hires them to maintain the road. That wasn't important to Roy when his horses Minnie and Buster were alive. The old team "could follow a snow-covered trail and never step off. Anything you'd hook them to, they'd try to pull."

Roy milks five cows twice a day; the cream goes to a collecting station in Montrose. His nine-year-old dog, Boots, brings in the cows. "She just takes off and gets them moving in. She'll start two or three walking and the rest follow, real slow like. Boots likes the stock, and won't bite unless a cow steps on her."

We walked through the corral to see Creamo, Roy's palomino saddle horse, and continued to the chicken house, where Sarah collected eggs from the 250 hens. "She won't let me do it," Roy said. "She's afraid I'd break them."

As cold as it gets in winter, Roy likes the early spring less. The thaw means problems. "That doggone mud is the worst of all," he said, using the harshest language I heard during my visit. "You can't do anything. You can't go anywhere.

"Summer is my favorite time. I can see things grow."

On the 630 acres to the east, Edwin

and Donna rear three children who no longer go to Sanborn Park School. Anita, 15, and Ernie, 14, are in high school in Norwood, so Donna also drives 12-year-old Tom to school there.

One such daily trip nearly proved fatal in April 1972. The steep, narrow, rutted dirt road has many cliffside switchbacks. Donna was driving the children home in the family's two-seat pickup truck when a steering column tie-rod broke on a turn.

Down the slope plunged the vehicle, tumbling and sliding for 150 feet to a ledge, then down another 20 feet before coming to rest. Miraculously, the children suffered only a few painful bumps, Donna a bruised arm. She climbed back up to the road and walked three miles home for help. The pickup was a total loss; so were three big trees that helped slow its descent.

Despite hard work and some hazards and inconveniences, the families of Sanborn Park are enthusiastic about their life and location in one of nature's choice recreation areas. Skiing, riding, fishing, finding Indian arrowheads—the things that visitors come to their high country to do—are part of their routine.

"We realize how lucky we are that we can make a living in the place we most want to be," said Ella Marolf. "When I smell the sun on the pine needles, I just can't imagine living anywhere else."

Colorado has 53 peaks that rise above 14,000 feet. Pikes Peak, at 14,110, is undoubtedly the best known, but there are 32 that are higher.

In the geographical center of the state is the high, open expanse called South Park. The majestic peaks that surround it have to be giants to be impressive, for the Park County seat of Fairplay is itself at an elevation of 9,990 feet.

Early-day hunters used the word *park* to refer to high, broad mountain valleys where large numbers of game animals—buffalo, antelope, deer, and elk—congregated. South Park was one of these —a flat, grassy basin, 50 miles north to south, 35 miles wide.

Winter begins in South Park in August, say the residents, and ends in July.

It has been known to snow in every month of the year. Around the windy, treeless expanse, lofty peaks stand like sentinels: Lincoln, Sherman, Buckskin, Bross, Pennsylvania, Horseshoe, Sheep, Buffalo, Silverheels.

In 1859 a group of gold prospectors, driven away from the rich placers at a place named Tarryall, set up their own camp on the Middle Fork of the South Platte River and named it Fairplay, to distinguish it emphatically from the place they damned as "Graball." By 1872 Fairplay was an incorporated town, the county seat, and the center of the region's mining activity.

Fairplay — population 404 — is still South Park's major town. Most of the mines have been shut down for almost a generation, there's no industry, and a visitor wonders how the several stores on Front and Main Streets survive.

The area's ranches, summer homes, and tourism are part of the reason Fairplay lives on. So are Kay Pocock, Arlene Coil, and Edith Teter, natives who are devoted to their town. And there are newcomers like Mather Wallis and his wife, Joan, who are equally loyal. The Wallises left the East Coast to take over the *Park County Republican & Fairplay Flume*, established in 1879; they publish every Thursday, using a 1908 Mergenthaler Linotype and an even older flatbed, eight-page press.

Fairplay has a few other things going for it, too. It is the self-proclaimed Burro Capital of the World. It has South Park City, a remarkable restoration of a one-street Colorado mining town, full of authentic old buildings, equipment, furniture, pictures, and artifacts. And every fall when the aspens turn to gold, Fairplay's slopes are gloriously colorful.

The price paid to live in this high country is usually a lot of hard work. Mrs. Teter, 70, still teaches in the Fairplay School, as she has off and on for two generations. The petite Mrs. Pocock works for a title company; her husband, Bob, runs a grocery store. Mrs. Coil helps her husband, Walter, on their sheep and cattle ranch.

(Continued on page 154)

Lounging on the back of her father's favorite stallion, Five-or-Nine, 12-year-old Bonnie Kettle daydreams with her sister Marnie on a lazy summer afternoon. The girls represent the fourth generation of Kettles to live on the 6,000-acre San Isabel Ranch in the Wet Mountain Valley of Colorado. Their father, Dr. Ben Kettle (right), manages a prize herd of more than a thousand registered Herefords with the help of his family and two hired hands. Celebrating the ranch's 100th anniversary in 1972, the Kettles played hosts for the annual field day of the Colorado Junior Hereford Association. Above, several members of the family spruce up the sign at the ranch entrance.

Pack train of elk hunters edges up a chaparral-covered hillside as a freight train passes through Colorado's Glenwood Canyon. Engineer Harvey Cline (below) watches from the cab; autumn aspens blur past the window as his locomotive helps haul a train up the steep grade to 10,242-foot Tennessee Pass on the Continental Divide. Six extra diesels in tandem, controlled by two enginemen, join each freight at the town of Minturn for the 21-mile climb. The half-dozen "helper-unit" crewmen stationed here call themselves the Minturn Hillbillies.

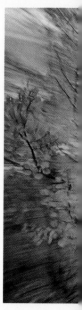

Snowflakes and drifting steam partially obscure a bull elk resting near a thermal pool in the West Thumb, Wyoming, area of Yellowstone National Park. Although such warm basins provide refuge for animals during the bitterly cold winter, most elk migrate to lower elevations; the bones in the foreground probably belonged to an aged elk unable to keep up with the herd. Above, a coyote trots across an expanse of snow in search of the scent of potential prey. In the Rockies, as in other mountain regions, settlers relied on wild animals as a source of food and clothing. "Even today," says photographer Bruce Dale, "mountain people have a special appreciation for wildlife. Since they share the same environment, the animals become a part of the mountain dweller's life."

Mrs. Pocock recalls that donkeys ran loose in the town when she was a child. She never heard them called burros then.

"They were left over after all the mines closed," she said. "If you could catch one—I used a piece of bread—you could ride all day, or hitch it to a cart."

Donkeys or burros, the shaggy animals were invaluable in pioneer times. They were tough, strong, and surefooted, required little food, and performed a multitude of tasks in and out of the mines. And they seemed to enjoy human companionship. Because of their distinctive braying, miners affectionately labeled them Rocky Mountain canaries or Colorado mockingbirds.

Fairplay continues to honor their contribution to western history. On Front Street stands a monument to Prunes, a burro that lived to 63 years of age and worked in every mine in the district. And every July, the town hosts the World Championship Pack Burro Race.

"Kids still have it pretty good here," Kay Pocock said. "It's the freedom to come and go and not worry. Everyone looks out for everyone else. You know all the people. It's a good feeling, knowing help is always there if it's needed.

"When I was in the ninth grade, my aunt took me to eastern Colorado, near the Kansas line. There was a bigger school there. I stayed until Christmas, but I was really homesick for the mountains. So I came back to Fairplay, and I've been here ever since."

Constantly surrounded by high peaks on her 5,000-acre ranch, Arlene Coil admits that she gets to taking them for granted. "Then a stranger says, 'Oh, aren't they beautiful!' and I really look at them again—and they *are*, of course.

"Living on a ranch up here is rough, but I hate the city—too many people. When I start to wish our town had more shopping facilities, I realize that would bring in more people—and that would spoil Fairplay."

Arlene's great-great-uncle, Dave Miller, homesteaded in South Park in 1870. Kay's grandfather, John Moran, was an early-day miner. The two girls grew up together, and they are still best friends.

Grazing as they walk, sheep slowly move from summer range 11,000 feet high in the mountains above Minturn to fall pastures at a lower elevation. Mounted and armed, herder Samson Haron, a Basque who came from the Pyrenees mountains of France 20 years ago, guides the flock—a thousand ewes with their lambs—belonging to J. Perry Olson, owner of a large cattle and sheep ranch near Wolcott, Colorado. As winter sets in, trucks will carry the animals 200 miles to desert range. In a year's migration the sheep may cover more than 500 miles. The weathered face of Dale Williams (opposite) reflects his long years as a Colorado sheepman. At 65, he still manages a flock of 1,200 sheep in partnership with his son, Danny.

Steering a homemade forklift he pieced together from spare parts, Sam Yetter stacks rough logs at his 5-Y Lumber Company near Meeteetse, Wyoming. "He's good at 'mechanicking,'" says Sam's wife, Clara. "We haven't done much lumbering lately because we can't buy trees from the Forest Service. So we pitch in doing other things." Below, she pauses while clearing away the remains of an old barn. Sometimes Clara drives a grader on a stretch of mountain road.

Like most old mining towns, Fairplay has its share of gutted foundations and abandoned buildings intermingled with the active business houses. Main and Front are the only paved streets. The town's modest homes have plenty of yard space between them. Everything isn't old; the community is very proud of the modern junior-senior high school, and of the spacious new county hospital.

Edith Teter teaches high school English just eight miles from the Black Mountain ranch where she was born, and only a few blocks from the Fairplay home where she gave birth to her two sons. She knows everybody in town; most of her former students, however, have left Fairplay.

"Youngsters with a college education — what would they have here?" she asked. "Kids know what they want, and they go out and get it. Fairplay never will be a boom town, unless mining is revived. Tourism alone won't do it. There are more summer homes, but those people don't stay during the school year. People who stay are the working people."

Mrs. Teter stays — and works. "I'm too busy to leave in the winter, and it's too nice in the summer." Along with her teaching she keeps house for her bachelor son, Roy, who manages their 1,100-acre ranch southwest of town. The other son, George, is an aircraft designer and lives with his family in California.

"Roy hires four men for haying, and I cook for the crew," she said. "I have fun, too. Michigan Creek flows through the ranch, and I like to fish. I don't much care for eating trout, but I do like to fish."

Mrs. Teter rarely has more than 20 students in a class. The small classes are obviously an advantage, and in fact she doesn't think South Park children in the 1970's are disadvantaged in any way.

"I believe today's communications equalize everything," she said. "Books, television, newspapers, magazines, ready transportation — nobody's boxed in. The students here can get four TV channels on the cable and see everything the Denver kids do."

In the mountains, the conversation always seems to get back to the weather:

"We had a little snow on the Fourth of July," she said, but added that the summer really was very pleasant. "We never do have any spring—it's just too cold too long up here."

In the old saloon on Front Street now occupied by the *Fairplay Flume,* editor Mather Wallis was plotting a way to increase circulation by persuading summer residents to keep up on the news all winter—by mail. That raised the question: What news is there in the wintertime?

Mather always starts by checking with the town's policeman and with its only doctor. Sometimes he has to scratch hard for a subject for his weekly column, "Out of the Flume." Once in late fall he was reduced to interviewing an aspen, and reported that the tree was not quaking, it was shivering with cold.

From South Park the Continental Divide sweeps northward through Rocky Mountain National Park before turning west. At Muddy Pass, before the Divide curves north again toward Wyoming, a lonely road leads into an even more isolated basin surrounded by 12,000-foot mountains, lower but no less beautiful than those guarding South Park.

This is North Park, actually more accessible from Wyoming than from Colorado. About 1,800 people live in its 1,600 square miles—half of them in Walden, the Jackson County seat—enclosed by the Continental Divide on the west and south, the Medicine Bow Mountains on the east and north.

Evelyn Brinker has spent all her 65 years in North Park. Since 1951 she has been postmistress of Coalmont, Colorado, present population zero. Nobody lives in Coalmont anymore, but the post office still serves some 40 rural families.

Once Coalmont was a thriving community and railroad terminal. The tracks were pulled up years ago, and there isn't even a general store left. But there's daily activity in Mrs. Brinker's small frame building, for she is not only postmistress but close friend to her patrons, all of whom call her Brinky and drop by as often as they can.

"It's a long trek to anywhere in the

Grizzled mountain man Anson Eddy leans on a hitching rail hung with traps outside his log cabin near the Buffalo Bill Reservoir in Wyoming. A trapper and hunter most of his 80 years, he still guides hunting parties in search of elk, bighorn sheep, and grizzly bears. "Eddy belongs to that handful of leathery pioneers we have left in the West," said a longtime friend. "He is one of a passing generation." Eddy claims to have served with the Royal Canadian Mounted Police as a young man. Friends acknowledge he has had his share of adventures and controversies; two bullet holes (right) in a window of his house resulted from one disagreement.

wintertime," she told me, "so the post office serves as a gathering place and general information center. I dread to think about when there'll be nothing left of Coalmont."

Brinky handles her duties with dispatch and efficiency despite the loss of her right leg about 15 years ago. Several operations for osteomyelitis culminated in amputation above the knee. She cannot use an artificial leg, but she moves everywhere on her crutches, drives a car, and zips around her office on a chair fitted with rollers.

She opens for business promptly at 10 a.m., after slowly running the American flag up the pole outside the building. At noon she closes for lunch and drives to her home two miles away, then reopens until 5 p.m.

Aside from an abandoned schoolhouse, the post office is almost all that's left of Coalmont. Evidence of the coal-mining past remains—water-filled pits, weatherbeaten shacks, bizarre sinkholes, and, in winter, occasional open patches in the snow indicating long-smoldering fires underground. When Brinky pinpoints a burning coal vein, she notifies U. S. Bureau of Mines officials in Denver and they send earth-moving equipment to try to smother it.

Rolling about her office, Brinky plunks the mail into the old wooden cubicles, wields her hand-cancellation stamp, and talks about the job she'll never resign (she will have to retire at 70) and the country she'll never leave.

"I was born over on the east side of the park on the Canadian River," she said. "We were right against the mountains and had lots of trees. When I first saw Coalmont I thought it was the end of creation."

In 1929 she married Elmer Brinker, who had homesteaded 160 acres west of Coalmont. They still live there in a house that faces the majestic Park Range; the south fork of Little Grizzly Creek runs below her kitchen window. Except for the house next door—where her son, daughter-in-law, and three grandchildren live—there isn't a neighbor in sight.

"I look at the mountains a lot, and the beautiful sky," she said. "Sometimes in winter the reflection of the sky makes the snow look blue."

The wind out of Wyoming, she admitted, could get pretty violent. How violent? She pointed to a 40-foot, heavy steel antenna on her son's roof that had been twisted like a pretzel.

Her husband, Elmer, sometimes sits in for Brinky. Several years ago he made a remarkable recovery from a stroke, and at 83 again is active. Born in Fort Collins, he came to North Park in 1911 for a haying job and stayed on. For 15 years he was superintendent of a coal mine.

Elmer is one of North Park's biggest boosters. "I like the climate, and anytime I can get off in the woods I'm happy. It's sure not as tough living here as down there in Denver. When I was younger, the deeper the snow was the better I liked it. When you're young, it seems you can do anything."

Brinky's black hair is graying; her lined face reflects years of pain. After she suffered a heart attack several years ago, her doctor urged her to move to a lower elevation. "No, I won't do that," she said to me. "Nowhere else has the peace we have here."

West of Chugwater, Wyoming, in the Laramie Mountains, I visited Cora and Duncan Grant in the two-story sandstone house he helped his Scottish immigrant father build in 1889. It is only a few miles from the site of the log cabin in which he was born 91 years ago.

I arrived on a December day when the wind was howling—a good day to stay indoors, I thought—but I found Duncan chopping wood for the kitchen range. His hair is white, but his complexion is ruddy and his physique is still rugged. "I feel like 65," he boasted when I remarked on the strenuous work he was doing. He did make a concession on his 90th birthday, he said: He gave up horseback riding, blaming an old knee injury, and he agreed to let his son, Robert, relieve him of irrigating the hayfields. Other than that, he decided, he would continue as active boss of the 20,000-acre cattle operation.

Dunc drives a pickup truck around the ranch, but he stays off main highways because "I don't see the rocks as well as I used to." He doesn't wear glasses, though. Most of the time he feels no need for them; from a lifetime of association he knows every foot of the country from the Richeau Hills to the Medicine Bow Mountains.

Long ago, winter and summer for five years, he and his brother, Bob, were paid to ride those hills and kill wolves. Just before the turn of the century, an estimated 10,000 big gray wolves threatened the high-country cattle industry. Swan Land & Cattle Co., predecessor of today's Two Bar Ranch Co., equipped the brothers with new Winchester 1894 smokeless-powder .30-30 rifles and agreed to pay $8 for each adult wolf's hide, $2.50 for a pup's.

Dunc showed me a white scar on his left wrist, and then walked over to the flared window of the living room. There were still Indian scares in Wyoming when the house was built, and the window casings were shaped so a rifleman could stand out of direct line of sight and still have a wide angle from which to fire. Dunc pointed out toward the hills.

"We discovered a den up on a high ridge, about 40 miles west of Chugwater Creek in the Laramie Mountains," he recalled. "The hole went straight into the hillside.

"I had my Colt .38 six-shooter in my right hand and my carbide lamp in the left as I crawled in. Bob waited outside. I was about ten feet into the den when I saw a wolf four or five feet in front of me. I shot it in the head.

"I set down the lamp to pull the dead wolf out and skin it. I didn't notice a small tunnel to my left. As I reached forward, another wolf grabbed my wrist in its teeth. It was like a vise, getting tighter and tighter as I yelled and tried

Transparent stream flowing from Hanging Lake tumbles past moss-covered rocks in the shadows of Glenwood Canyon, Colorado.

to back out. I was afraid to shoot because I might hit myself in the arm.

"I dragged that live wolf all the way outside. Bob caved in its skull with a hammer, and still its jaws were locked on my arm. We finally got it loose after breaking off one of its teeth in my wrist. That hurt worse than anything in my life; I had to use a pocket knife to cut out the tooth—a good half-inch long. I bled pretty good."

In five years Dunc and Bob totaled some 250 wolf hides, but that was the only time either was bitten. Dunc still has the old lamp, revolver, and rifle, and brought them out to show to me.

All the time we were talking, the wind hadn't let up for a moment; but the great cottonwood trees on the north side of the house provided a good windbreak, just as Dunc's father intended when he planted them in the early 1890's.

Duncan is Platte County's oldest citizen, and when the *Wyoming Stockman-Farmer* celebrated its 75th anniversary the editor ran a picture of him "and my young wife" (she's 16 years his junior) on the cover. He's proud of that.

"I was never much for traveling out of Wyoming, but I did get to Iowa once," he said. "If I didn't think Wyoming was the best, I wouldn't have stayed here so long."

He enjoys driving up to his high pastures and showing the productive land that yields tons of sweet clover and native grass. "We had almost a barnful of hay left over last winter," he said.

Living by the sun, not by clocks, looking back on a long and satisfying life, enjoying the hours with his wife and their children, eight grandchildren, and three great-grandchildren, Duncan Grant reminded me of many I have known in the high valleys of the Rockies. Far from being overpowered by that vast mountain range, they have carved out a special, private world of security and beauty. They appreciate the land and the seasons. They adapt. They don't complain. They laugh freely and often. They know that they are privileged.

I never met a mountaineer that didn't teach me something. I guess that's why I keep going back.

Freckled 10-year-old Carol Ann Irvine rests hands and chin on a school desk in Sanborn Park, Colorado. Dried native flowers border a watercolor by Ella Marolf, depicting the one-room school her children attend along with Carol and her brother. Because of heavy winter snows, the youngsters take their vacation from January through March, and attend class all summer.

5

The Far West: "There's always another day"

by Stephen Wennstrom

THE PAVEMENT ENDS at the hamlet of Copper, and from there only a dirt track leads on into the Siskiyou Mountains of southwestern Oregon, through a forest of towering Douglas firs and ponderosa pines, to where Glen Young lives. Much of the road is too narrow for two cars; more than once I had to retreat several hundred feet to let someone past, observing the custom of mountain driving that the car heading uphill is the one that backs to a wider spot. In places the shoulder was crumbling and the road threatened to fall into the stream below.

So I was unprepared for the newly erected real estate sign as I rounded a bend several miles along the way: "One 5-acre tract, one 21-acre tract, creek and road frontage." Large and white, with bold red and black letters, the sign stood in startling contrast to its surroundings, and my first thought was for Glen. I knew he had come to this country before there were roads, that he cherished his privacy, and that the sign presaged changes he would deplore.

Parking in his yard, I paused before getting slowly out of the car, trying to think of something to spend a couple of minutes doing, knowing Glen would already be watching me to determine whether I was friend or stranger and deciding whether he wanted to talk today. Maybe he's across the stream, I thought, working his gold mine, or maybe he's in the house reading; in any event, he already knows I'm here. You don't sneak up on him.

Presently he emerged from indoors, wearing his quizzical smile. "Well, here's the National Geographic again," he chuckled. "I didn't figure you'd be back. You know everything I tell you is lies. Come on in."

Glen Young is a ruddy, robust bear of a man who exudes health and—to friends—good cheer; with strangers he is much more reserved. He is graying and he stoops slightly now—"I've shrunk some from my six feet two, you know"—but his durable frame, clear eyes, and seemingly unlimited energy belie his 86 years. I would have guessed him to be 60, perhaps 65 at the outside.

Glen has been operating his mining claim for more than 40 years. He goes to town — Jacksonville — only when necessary, and keeps a six-month supply of food and other necessities in case, for some reason, he should be unable to get out. Until about five years ago his boon companion was his wife, Florence — whom he consistently refers to simply as Wife. "There was never a harsh moment between us," he once said to me. Since her death he has left the place even less frequently.

I noticed patches of flowers scattered here and there in the shade of the tall conifers. "Wife always had a garden," he explained, "and these are leftovers. It's so rocky here that we had to haul soil to wherever she wanted to plant something. We must've moved tons of dirt."

Despite his long tenure in these highlands, Glen doesn't consider himself a true "mountain man." He reserves that term for the old hunters and trappers who ranged deep into the high country and seemingly never settled down. "The real mountain men were wanderers," he said. "Nobody knew where they lived or when they might be comin' down. They used to stop by to visit us — Wife, mostly, she was a great talker. Once when she went down to get the mail she fell into conversation with a group of the roughest men you could imagine. If I'd known they were camped down there, I never would've let her go. But you know, when she got back she was all excited about some new recipes she was itchin' to try. 'All they wanted to talk about was cooking,' she said. 'There wasn't a coarse word spoken.' After that they used to stop by to gossip with her on their way to town or back."

Recalling the new real estate sign, I asked Glen whether he'd considered moving farther back into the hills, to put more distance between himself and the nearest neighbor. "Sure, I've thought about it," he said sadly. "But there's no 'back' any more. I used to be at the end of that road out there, but now it goes 50 miles farther up, and on weekends the place is crawling with tourists, driving

(Continued on page 170)

Rushing waters of the Yuba River run past deserted rocks once crowded with eager forty-niners panning for gold. Collectors in Nevada City, California, own the nuggets and the set of scales.

Pegleg Creek in the Sierra north of Placerville, California, tempts 72-year-old Roy Arling to try his luck. With his dog and battered pickup truck, the lifelong prospector follows his instincts from stream to stream, moving into any shelter available. A small pension and the money he makes panning gold satisfy his modest wants; a trip to town once a month breaks the solitude. Beside the creek a cheering fire warms hands and coffeepot. Rubber gloves give protection from the icy water, muddied by the swirling in the pan. The gravel yields a tiny nugget, worth about a dollar.

Solitude for the spirit lures pilgrims
to the Ananda Cooperative Community
near Nevada City, California. About
20 people live year around at the 72-acre
retreat, meditating and studying the
teachings of yoga. A laughing mother
lifts her daughter during a May Day
celebration at Ananda. Nearby, in the
cooperative's reservoir, a young
swimmer spouts like a whale. Its
leaders, who founded the retreat in 1966,
forbid use of hallucinogenic drugs and
alcohol. Residents raise their own
crops for vegetarian meals. Visitors find
a welcome from May through October,
and can rent cabins or campsites.

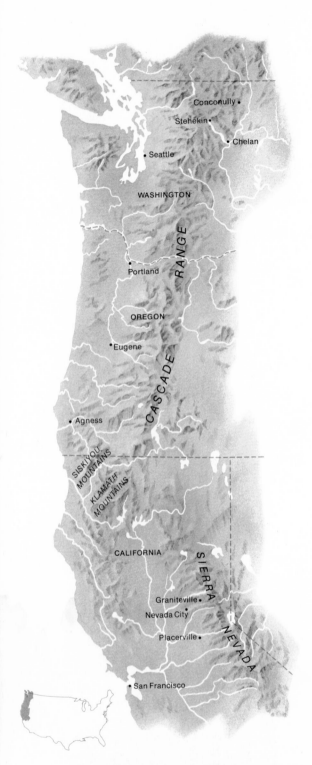

Forbidding barriers during the westward movement, the rugged mountains of the Far West—Sierra Nevada, Cascades, lower ranges near the coast—still contain vast areas of splendid wilderness.

jeeps, looking for a place to fish or whatever they do. Now, with the snowmobiles, they come all winter, too."

On my earlier visits I had always run out of time, and had never had a thorough tour of Glen's property, so I asked him to show me around. I did know about his washing machine. Since he has no electricity he has rigged it with a simple water turbine, called by miners a Pelton wheel, driven by the creek that runs through the yard. The roof section of an old car body shelters the works. I walked over for a closer look. "Tablespoons," Glen chuckled with obvious pride. "I built that turbine with tablespoons and the flywheel from an old Lincoln."

When I asked about his mine, Glen suggested that we walk to the dam he had built farther up the creek. Climbing the steep trail was hard work. Whenever we stopped to rest for a moment, Glen would point out another feature of the stream bed or the hillside:

"This here is an old ditch, dug by a couple of guys who were minin' around the hill. Runs about a quarter mile.

"Over there's where some fellows have been takin' out serpentine for sculptures. Two cents a pound, I charge them, and they're tickled to get it for that, but they do all the cuttin' and haulin' so it's pure profit for me."

On a ridge opposite the cabin, we passed his open-air blacksmith shop. "Oh, sure, I do a little blacksmith work. I can even weld pretty good with heat and hammer on that thing," he said, pointing to his anvil.

A trace of a smile creased his weathered face as he told me of the times that people had carried off his tools. Once someone even stole a large anvil. "Can you imagine luggin' that heavy thing down the mountain?" he laughed. I shook my head in wonder, both at the motivation of the thieves and at the magnanimity of their victim. He had told me other stories of mysterious theft and vandalism, but he always seemed to distill more humor than bitterness out of such situations.

When we finally arrived at the dam, Glen explained the massive 6-by-12-foot headgate which automatically controls the flow of the stream. "It's one of those bumblebee kind of things," he mused. "You know, a bumblebee's not supposed to be able to fly, say the scientists, and this rig isn't supposed to be able to function." No amount of calculation and advice from engineering consultants could have designed the mechanism Glen had built, I am certain. "But it works," he said, "and it's actually the simplest darn thing you can imagine."

Having given up trying to draw a plan for the headgate, Glen developed his idea through models. The full-scale version controls the level of a million-gallon reservoir through a complex combination of floats, cables, levers, and hand-hewn timbers. The dam-and-reservoir system provides water for his house and mining operation, waterpower for the Pelton wheel on the washing machine, and flood control—a spillway blasted out of solid rock helps channel off overflow.

"I used to figure to rebuild the thing every two years," Glen told me, "but this one's goin' on nearly eight now. Some of the boards are startin' to rot, so it'll need some work soon."

Lately he has been required to restrict his gold mining because of the silt discharged by his one-man operation. He insisted to me that such decisions, based on current concerns with ecological problems, were shortsighted and the result of incomplete information, and predicted that they would be tempered in time. "It's a fad," he said. "It'll blow over when people discover that everyone's income is tied to some kind of industry. When people get hungry enough they'll be reasonable about the whole thing. One good rainstorm puts more mud in the creek than all the miners do in years."

I didn't attempt to argue with him. He knew as well as I did that his interpretation of the situation was oversimplified and one-sided; but of course it was his livelihood that was affected.

Back at the cabin we fell to talking about the book on which Glen and Florence had collaborated, a sort of family journal that traces the lives and times of various kin. He seemed to have no interest in finding out what a publisher might

think of it—either for satisfactions of authorship or possible monetary return. "People tell me I ought to sell my book," he said, "but I don't see why. I've got what I want.

"Well, here we are sittin' and talkin' all afternoon, and you've stayed till suppertime. I suppose I have to feed you," he said with mock annoyance, his eyes betraying his pleasure. I promptly stood up and followed him into the house.

As distinctive an individualist as Glen Young is, he nevertheless is representative of certain mountaineers I encountered all through the high country of the Far West. They support themselves in a variety of ways: Some are miners, some are small farmers or ranchers, some are pensioners, some seem to eke out a subsistence from a garden and a few chickens and not much else. But what is important to all of them is elbow room, fresh air, a view of mountains and trees and running water, freedom from traffic and crowds and schedules: a sense of independence that has little to do with financial status.

And you have to be willing to travel some of the worst roads in the country in order to reach them.

The road to George Wright's place south of Pinehurst, Oregon, is so rough that for almost three miles the speedometer needle hung at zero as my beetle of a car crept around boulders and ruts. Several times I was tempted to abandon the road altogether in favor of the open ground on either side.

The country is a rolling, high plateau section of the Klamath Mountains, more sparsely forested than the Siskiyous and less green. Here and there the ponderosa pines give way to scrub oaks, chaparral, and open meadows.

The weathered, unpainted house and barn of the Wright place sit among the willows beside Skookum Gulch, almost surrounded by a rail fence. Chickens and guineas patrolled the yard, and a bantam hen hurriedly gathered her chicks together to guard them from me, but not a human was in sight. As I stood watching the conscientious hen I heard a faint

"Halloo" from the hill above the house. "Come on up," George Wright called in welcome. "It's cooler up here."

George's father homesteaded this ground in 1881, and George has lived here all his 75 years except for a period during boyhood when he stayed with relatives nearer school. When he was a young man, he used to take short-term outside jobs to earn money, mostly driving cattle down to California ranches or markets, but his absences from the high country of Oregon's Klamaths were always temporary.

George still has no driver's license, and he has never been in an airplane. The longest trip he ever made was on horseback, with a friend, "over to the mining country in the Siskiyou Mountains. We were going prospectin'. We never found any gold, but we sure saw some pretty country, especially down on the Rogue around Agness."

When I asked if there is any place he would like to go to live or to visit, he seemed mildly amused. "Nope, I guess not," he said with a smile. "I'm satisfied right here."

Apparently he did give my question some further thought, for later he added, "Of course, I haven't looked around much. Maybe in another 25 years or so I'll be lookin' for another place, ready to start over."

When we walked up to the spring from which George draws drinking water during the dry summer months, we passed extensive agate beds where rock hounds come to search for the handsome stones. They arrive in jeeps and camper vans, some from distant states, and pay George a small fee to dig. The road and stream bed were littered with golfball-size agates of various hues, rejects from the diggers' discoveries.

But of more interest to George than agates are the yampa plants—George calls them "apaws"—that grow in abundance on his land. Indians used to visit this area every summer to harvest yampa tubers, a staple of their diet for a good part of the year, and George learned from them how to dig and use the plants.

"The squaws would come first," he recalled, "and they'd dig for several weeks. Then the men would show up to help haul the load back."

George obviously admired the Indians he had known. "They were good people, honest and generous. Some of the same ones came year after year, and we got to be friends."

Intrigued by his descriptions of "apaws" and wild onions, I asked if it would be possible to find a few.

"Sure, there's an apaw right over there," he said, pointing to a tall, white-flowered plant. We dug a few of the small tubers; they had a flavor like moist hazel nuts, surprisingly sweet. We looked in vain for wild onions, but George assured me that in the spring they are all over the place.

Power transmission lines cross the property, but George has never attempted to get electricity connected to his house. "You take a feller like me that's never had it," he replied, "we don't need it, don't miss it, afraid of it, no use for it, don't even want it around." He concentrated for a minute, trying to think of some justification in his life for electricity, but couldn't seem to come up with any. He did allow that the refrigerator "comes in handy, but it runs on propane."

I discovered that my host, despite the limits of his own travels, has an intense interest in politics and world affairs—admittedly with a certain detachment. He is philosophical about social and economic problems in the manner of someone who simply doesn't rely much on money. "No, the Depression didn't hurt me much. I dug around," he said. "In the cities, that's where they got hurt. But I'd rather see a depression than a war. It learned people a lot. When people got ahold of something they hung onto it; when they got a little money they would buy something they really needed, not spend it on darn foolishness."

George keeps track of national political affairs by listening to his battery radio. He tried to enlist me as his campaign manager in case he should decide to run for President. "I want to start from the top and work down, not the other way around," he said with a grin.

I found myself almost immediately at ease with George Wright, partly no doubt because he seemed comfortable with me, even when pauses and extended silences befell our conversations. Obviously he did not feel obliged to entertain me; but he also wanted me to know I was not imposing. "Don't think you're takin' up my time, because you're not," he said.

George's watch always shows what he calls "old-time," not that "newfangled daylight-savin' business." He willingly translates for anyone who asks the time, but he sees no point in moving the hands ahead an hour in the spring and back again in the fall.

He had his last three teeth pulled about six years ago. He would much rather be without teeth than to run the risk of a toothache, he said. "You ever have a toothache? Man, there's nothing like it. I told the dentist, 'This here's the last time I'm comin' to see you. If you want to see me you'll have to come out to my place.' He figured maybe he'd fix me up with dentures, but I said no, I'd get along. Eatin' takes more time than tools, and I got lots of time."

When we sat down to venison steak, cooked squash and onions, potato salad, fresh tomatoes, and pork and beans, I soon realized that the lack of teeth didn't slow George down much. "Most people just get false teeth for looks anyway," he said, "keep 'em in their pocket most of the time."

A durable composure shines through his clear blue eyes, and his wry sense of humor helps him deal with things beyond his control or understanding. He seemed to me a man without frustrations, living in the manner he prefers, free of ambitions and desires he cannot fulfill.

*T*ime seems unimportant to most mountain people. I found no one in a hurry, and more than once I heard the comment, "If we don't get to it now, there's always another day."

Photographer Bruce Dale and I got a lesson in mountain time while visiting Roy Arling, who prospects in the Sierra Nevada north of Placerville, California. We had agreed to meet Roy at Pegleg

Roadside sign near Pinehurst, Oregon, warns away visitors. Some western mountain people cling to their isolation, resisting and retreating before the advances of urbanization.

Creek to try some placer mining; he had told us to go on ahead, adding that he would be along "in half an hour or so."

We waited more than two hours at Pegleg, and when there was still no sign of the 72-year-old prospector we became concerned for his safety and drove the six miles back to his place. There he was, still sorting shovels and picks, surprised to see us and amused at our discomfiture. "You fellows get lost?" he asked.

As it turned out, there was yet more sorting and then an impromptu nap before Roy was ready to go. We were to learn that Roy never got too involved in anything to lie down—wherever he happened to be, without prologue or apology —for a 20-minute nap.

With our pickup-load of tools and old boards, we built a dam and sluice box in order to work a seam in the rocks that Roy thought promising. There followed several hours of labor with pick and shovel, then some sluicing and panning, punctuated by Roy's occasional bursts of impatience at our awkwardness: "I don't see how a guy can go to college and not know more than that about how to pan gold," he grumbled at one point.

Finally we were rewarded with a few specks of yellow metal. Accustomed by now to his no-nonsense manner and eager for commendation, we hurried to show Roy our precious find.

His appraisal was quick. "Now put that in that other bucket, over there," he ordered, obviously well aware of the work-stopping fever that often overcomes the novice gold-seeker with his first find. "Don't look at it too long," he snapped.

Reluctantly we did as we were told and went back to work, clumsily trying to imitate his practiced panning motion. But even as we improved I knew we could never duplicate his patience and determination.

As we came to know Roy we realized that his life-style preserves an "easy-come, easy-go" pattern typical of many a miner, cowboy, lumberman, and soldier of an earlier day: When you have it you spend it, and when it's gone you go back to work and pay full attention to the job. Roy told us that he goes to Placerville once a month to pick up his World War I pension check. His routine is always the same: He takes a room at a good hotel, enjoys a thorough bathing and barbering, fills his pockets with expensive cigars, and takes a friend to a favorite saloon and then out to supper. He continues to live in such comfort for several days until the money runs out. Then he goes back into the mountains, resumes his prospecting, and waits for the next pension check. If and when his gold panning turns an unusual profit, he can go to town without waiting for the check.

On a couple of occasions I had heard Roy referred to as "Down-the-Road Dugan," but it wasn't until a return visit that I found out why. As I drove up to his house the place looked abandoned; the clutter of tools and mining gear was gone from the yard, and the door was locked. From neighbors I learned that Roy had indeed moved on "down the road," taking up residence in another cabin 30 miles away. And the next time I saw him, Roy was traveling again, having loaded his incredible collection of equipment into his battered pickup truck and stationed Rex, his venerable black hound, on top of the pile as guard.

I thought of Glen Young's comment that the true mountain men were wanderers.

Graniteville, California, was a bustling mining town a century ago; nowadays its year-round population is only a half-dozen hardy souls, who remain snowed in through the Sierra winter without telephones or electricity.

One of them is Lester Poage, a native of Graniteville who went away to work for the Pullman Company for 26 years but returned to his hometown in 1945. Despite the long, lonely winters, Mr. Poage is acutely aware of the growing press of outsiders; for vacationists and real estate promoters have discovered the abandoned mining towns of California, and communities that have dozed peacefully for half a century or more are suddenly seeing their environs developed as parks, campgrounds, and vacation home sites. The impact on the mountain people, many of them lifelong residents, comes most often in the form of higher taxes, more regulations, more commotion, and increasing vandalism.

"Everybody's buttin' in, and what do we get for it? Just more expense," declared Mr. Poage. Yet he well understands the appeal of the mountains for urbanites, having returned from his long exile to live in the house built by his parents in 1880. He came back to escape the noise and confusion of city life, and he admits he has difficulty understanding those who willingly stay and brave the freeways every day. "They're just fightin' to get to work. What's the sense of that, anyway?"

On his front porch a 50-year-old pair of skis attests to his commitment to a slower pace; on them he delivered mail once a week to the winter residents of Graniteville from 1945 to 1955.

At the height of its mining boom almost a century ago, Graniteville boasted one of the world's first telephone lines. In 1878, only two years after Alexander Graham Bell first demonstrated his new invention in Boston, the Ridge Telephone Company installed a 60-mile line from French Corral, near Graniteville in Nevada County, to Milton in Sierra County, to serve companies engaged in hydraulic mining. The line remained in operation for more than 20 years.

Today the town is far more isolated than it was then, its roads indifferently maintained, its residents unreachable by phone. "There was 20 feet of snow here in 1952," recalls Mr. Poage, "and 18 feet in 1965, and there's always at least half that. Nobody bothers with the roads until about April.

"Now I realize that's an advantage. The question is, how to protect ourselves the rest of the year."

Although the western mountaineers live away from crowds and congestion by preference, they come together with enthusiasm for social and political gatherings. I arrived one evening in Conconully, Washington, in time for a public hearing on proposals to change the status of certain public lands. Accustomed to a tiny turnout of citizens at most public meetings in the cities where I have lived, I was surprised to find almost 40 people in the community hall. That was more than half of the adults living in the area, I was told, and they had come despite bitter cold and the fact that ice and snow made driving hazardous.

A fire was crackling in the potbellied stove at one side of the hall, and a giant urn of coffee sent its fragrance through the room. For more than two hours the group listened to the proposals, studied maps, asked questions, and expressed opinions in the tradition of the American town meeting. I found the degree of participation and the obvious sense of community remarkable.

More frequently, however, it is a celebration, contest, or social that brings mountain people together. At Agness, Oregon, the periodic turkey shoots are major events, drawing marksmen and their families from miles around.

Turkeys are the prizes, not the targets, and the competition gets extremely close. The shoot serves as an excuse for family picnics on the grass; after the turkeys have been claimed, the crowd moves to the community hall for bingo and other games, and a potluck supper.

Agness overlooks the Rogue River where it cuts through the Coast Range just above its confluence with the Illinois River, about 20 miles from the Pacific. One of the town's longtime residents is Len Blondell, an inveterate critic of government and public services who was reared near Big Stone Gap, Virginia. He still speaks of that part of the country with affection, and his accent is more Appalachian than western, but the transplanting seems to have taken: Len has been a fixture in the Agness community since 1930. For nearly 40 years he ran a pack-horse operation in the mountains around the town. Recently he has kept himself occupied with a few cattle, a garden, and his fruit trees. I never leave his place without being urged to take some of his fine figs or vegetables to my wife — and I never refuse. What Len can't eat or give away, he cans himself.

The vehemence Len displayed when talking about politicians abruptly disappeared when we started to discuss music, and he seemed genuinely pleased when I asked him to play his fiddle. Carefully getting down the battered case, he began to lament that he didn't have a better bow. "Don't know if we'll get much music from this," he said, peering critically at the bow while nestling the violin under his chin. "My best bow is gettin' fixed — guess he must've forgot to send it back. This old thing's about wore out. Made it myself out of that filament fishline stuff."

As he began to run the bow gently across the strings, his eyes softened. He took a while to warm up, occasionally playing a snatch of a tune, sometimes just filling in with runs and chords. "Know what that is?" he would interject at random; usually I failed him, and he seemed to enjoy my uncertainty. But gradually he became engrossed in the music and the memories, playing on and on, no longer speaking, not seeing or caring that the cat was into mischief again, that the sun was going down. Eventually he forgot that I was there, and the delicate tracery of the improvised music drifted out over the garden and pasture, seeming to complement the rhythms of trees and grass as they moved in the breeze.

For a long time we were both caught up in the music's spell. Finally Len stopped, and his arms sagged; a faint, slightly melancholy smile crossed his tanned face. "Don't play much anymore, I guess," he said, as if apologizing for being tired.

*I*t was in Agness that I learned some "young folks from the city" were living about six miles up the Illinois River. Nobody seemed to know exactly where they had come from or how long they had been there, but they were reported to be living on the old Briggs place, accessible only by trail.

As I hiked the six miles one June morning, some lines from Thoreau kept running through my mind: "I went to the woods because I wished to live deliberately, to front only the essential facts of life, and see if I could not learn what it had to teach...." And I wondered about these mountain newcomers I was going to visit. In many parts of the rural West in recent years I had already come across young people in communal groups and small family units, renting, squatting, buying, sharing small plots of land, trying to find an alternative to the bustle and population of cities, seeking a chance to pursue a simple, basic existence. Most I had met had seemed neither properly prepared or genuinely satisfied. Would these be any different?

As soon as I spied Leonard James, I thought perhaps they *were* different. I found him in his garden, his five-year-old daughter Tracey playing nearby. His welcome was warm, and it was immediately apparent that he knew a good deal about gardening.

"This is twice as big as last year's garden, and we've already been canning stuff from it," he explained with justifiable pride. He went on to tell me some of the things he had learned a few years earlier while working for an organic gardener in northern Oregon. "But I figure it'll take maybe five years to really get into the farming thing here, to know the seasons and soil and just how to do things."

As we talked we strolled down to a field near the river where Leonard's brother, Russell, was plowing a patch of ground to plant corn. He was operating a small tractor, ancient and temperamental, that had been brought in over the hiking trail by a prior tenant years before; the brothers had found that with a tune-up, some new belts, and considerable patience on the part of the driver, it performed remarkably well.

On the way down the slope we passed a large white horse grazing in the pasture. "That's Pal; he's been around this place for about ten years," Leonard said. "He knows the trails better than we do."

Pal, he added, carried in all supplies from Agness, including gasoline for the tractor and for a small engine recently installed to run a washing machine.

I was impressed by the Jameses' knowledge of the history of this place and the surrounding area. Leonard recounted

Cat named Goldie looks out from beneath the apron hem of her owner, Mrs. Eleanor Griffith, whose family has occupied the same farm near Kelsey, California, for more than 120 years. Her grandparents planted the daffodils.

tales and events as readily as one who had lived here all his life. Obviously he had talked eagerly to every old-timer he could find.

He had tried many kinds of retreats before coming to the mountains, he explained — city communes, desert meditational groups, and others — "but most of those people aren't sincere. Worse still, they don't know what they're doing." His conclusion had been that a closely knit family unit had much more chance of surviving under such conditions than a larger communal group, unless all the members of the commune were unusually responsible.

"One of the greatest things is the time I can spend with my children," he said. "When I had a town job, I came home tired and didn't pay much attention to the kids. But here they can be with me right while I'm working; they can really help, even though they're small, and they can learn right along with me."

At lunchtime I met his wife, Corky, and his younger daughter, Morning Song. Over vegetable stew and freshly made bread, I listened to Corky tell how she had learned to cook and to bake — neither of which she had ever done before — while coping with a wood range.

She and Leonard had developed a great interest in foods that grow wild. They had found dock, for example, in abundance around the farm, and neighbors had taught them how to use its leaves as greens, its seeds for meal, and the dried roots to make a healthful tea.

As we finished eating, the young couple explained that they soon would be leaving for a month or two so that Corky, whose baby was almost due, could enter the hospital at Gold Beach, at the mouth of the Rogue.

"Corky hasn't been to town in over a year now, and she really isn't looking forward to it," Leonard said. "Russell will take care of things here, and I'll have to get a temporary job to earn enough money for the doctor.

"Then we'll be back."

Retracing the forest trail to Agness, I felt certain the Jameses would be back. They seemed to belong here; they were obviously happy, they were willing to work, and they were extremely sensitive to their surroundings. That last factor, I realized, set them off from some of the mountain people I had met. For I had to admit that I had found a certain ambivalence among mountaineers in regard to matters of environment. Even on the superficial level many of them, like many of the rest of us, suffer split vision: They glory in the grandeur of the high country, its space and splendid vistas, while remaining oblivious to ugliness right at their feet. For the mountains are increasingly cluttered with everything from old car bodies to paper and plastic debris, contributed unfortunately by both residents and visitors. And many a dooryard is filled with what is doubtless considered a useful collection of dismantled machinery and equipment — indistinguishable, to a more objective eye, from a collection of junk.

At the philosophical level, the typical mountaineer again has contradictory attitudes. Fiercely independent, he resents having anyone tell him what he can or cannot do with his land; on the other hand, he tends to have a deep respect for the natural forces he has been dealing with for years, and a sincere desire to see the natural state preserved.

The old-timers have watched individual trees grow from seedlings to grand maturity, attuned themselves to the seasonal movements of wild creatures, accustomed themselves to the long cycles of drought and rain. Too often, they know, man's interference with nature has caused problems and then a compounding of problems, whether the motivation was to exploit or to repair.

Whatever the cultural influences of one mountain region upon another, some of the clues lie in music. Not long after the memorable afternoon on which Len Blondell played his violin for me, I learned that the National Oldtime Fiddlers' Contest and Festival was soon to take place in Weiser, Idaho.

Since I had planned a family trip to that part of the Northwest, I arranged

(Continued on page 194)

Surrounded by the majestic Cascades, the mail boat to Stehekin trails a wake on Lake Chelan.

Stehekin winter

NATURE DOMINATES and isolates Stehekin, Washington, throughout the year, but at no time more emphatically than in winter when the fair-weather visitors have gone.

On either side of the main cluster of cabins rise the mountains, bristling with dark green conifers and laden with snow. Northwestward the valley climbs gradually toward Cascade Pass in North Cascades National Park. Southeast of the settlement the glacial gorge of Lake Chelan, two miles at its widest, 1,500 feet at its deepest, stretches away 55 miles to the town of Chelan—a four-hour trip by mail boat, 25 minutes by floatplane. No telephone line reaches Stehekin. Radio provides a communications link, and a small hydroelectric plant supplies the village with power.

The 15 or 20 families that have settled here treasure certain things far more than most people do: the forest silence, soot-free snow, the scent of ponderosa pines, the chance to live a life as rustic as they wish.

The quiet weeks of winter vary little for them. Adults pursue a round of familiar duties. School, skiing, and playing in the snow break household routine for the children. Young and old alike look forward to the arrival of the mail boat, and to the occasional movie it brings from Chelan.

Chelan pilot Ernie Gibson, detained at Stehekin by a storm, struggles through foot-deep

water with a ladder in a nightlong effort to keep his plane's wings free of heavy snow.

Ray Courtney, a descendant of Stehekin's first settlers
in the 1890's, waits while his wife, Esther, takes hot
biscuits from the oven. Ray fills winter days by improving
the cabin he built and repairing equipment he uses as a
high-country guide in summer. Below, Peggy Ann Courtney
plods across a snowfield with photographer Bruce Dale's son
Christopher. With her boots hung up to dry, opposite, she
sits on the staircase her father hewed from a single log.

Students' skis on the porch and the teacher's snowmobile in the yard signal "school in session" at the one-room cabin three miles out of town. Eleven children of varying ages attend here, five girls and six boys. High school students enroll at Chelan, where they board with friends or relatives. Opposite, Clifford Courtney (left), his brother Mark, and Bobby Buhl team up at recess for a snowball fight. At right, Danny Wilsey eases into his ski bindings after class. Some of the youngsters ski five miles to school.

Wary but unafraid, two mule
deer show as little concern for
the photographer as for their
white crowns of snow crystals.
Some Stehekin residents
put out feed for deer in winter,
and the animals wander freely
through the community. In
season, however, they remain
legal game for hunters in Lake
Chelan National Recreation
Area though not in North
Cascades National Park.
The mountains around the lake
shelter wildlife in rich
variety, and in winter many
species migrate from higher
elevations to areas near the
shore. Passengers on boats
plying the lake commonly see
eagles, black bears, and
mountain goats as well as deer.

Fetching the Breeze family's daily water
supply, a young visitor lugs the last
two buckets from the icy creek toward
a sled he has loaded on the path. Half
a mile away sits the cabin Judy Breeze
shares with her daughter, Robbie, 11,
a son, Finley, 24, and family friends
who come and go year around. Wells
go dry when the water table falls in
winter, and the creeks become substitute
sources. Opposite, Robbie kneads bread
dough before placing it in pans to rise.
Finley guides one end of a crosscut
saw as he and a helper cut firewood.

Colorful patchwork contrasts with
winter white as Linda Trueman hangs
out a quilt she made, taking advantage
of a sunny day to air bedding and
dry laundry. Opposite, Pat Hutson
shovels snow from her roof while her
visiting father, Stan, works behind
her. Other roofs have steep pitches
to encourage accumulated snow to slide
off, but the builders of this one made
it flat with the intention of adding
another story. Lighted windows cast
their glow on deep snowdrifts
around the cabin of John Broussard,
a college professor on sabbatical leave.

Arrival of the mail boat almost
always draws a crowd to the
Stehekin landing, regardless of
weather. The boat runs Monday,
Wednesday, and Friday in winter
and daily in summer, bringing
mail, visitors, and the supplies
and library books townspeople
have ordered from Chelan. Ernie
Gibson's charter floatplane
and barges carrying heavy goods
also serve Stehekin. The general
store, several hundred yards from
the landing, contains the post
office—almost ensuring that
someone from every family will
drop by the store on mail day.
Bobby Buhl, below, wastes no time
in opening a letter from a friend.

to be there at the time of the festival.

Weiser was resounding with "string music." Fiddlers, guitarists, banjo and mandolin and dulcimer players had come to the little Idaho town from all over the country, with especially strong representation from the West and South. The competition continued for a full week, as the musicians reveled in the fervent, nostalgic music that in its own way documents so much of America's history.

Of even greater interest to me than the scheduled programs, however, were the spontaneous jam sessions going on all over town, impromptu music-making by all sorts of combinations of musicians, often strangers to one another. Far into the night they played, in the hotel ballroom, the packed lobby, the tree-lined parks, dozens of clusters of avid devotees of folk music.

Especially heartening was the number of young musicians, not budding professionals out to advance their careers but amateurs who had come for the love of the music, for what it says to them about life and roots and continuity, for the chance to hear and learn from the old-timers. Many of them were already amazingly good. I was particularly moved by a long, lean stringbean of a boy, no more than 12, who displayed exceptional skill as a fiddler. During an hour or more of nonstop improvising in the hotel lobby, he wore out two banjo players and all the guitarists who tried to keep up. When he finally lowered his fiddle to a burst of applause, his blush of embarrassment belied the confident maturity of his playing, and he was again the awkward, bashful country boy.

"Just keep goin' up this road till you cross Wolf Creek, then it's the next place," a neighboring farmer had told me. "You can't miss it."

I always smile at that friendly parting shot, because I know from experience that I *can* miss it. But despite two feet of snow I found the entrance to the mile-long driveway of the Ed Kikendalls near Winthrop, in Washington's northern Cascades.

My car made it up the long, snowy lane,

but when I started to walk to the back door of the house my way was blocked by a large milk cow standing placidly in the beaten path that ran between deep drifts. For a considerable time the cow and I stood there looking at each other, while I tried to think of a practical and dignified way to proceed. It was still a stand-off when Mr. Kikendall happened to come out of the house.

Without allowing himself a smile at my ineptitude, he apologized politely for his cow and began coaxing her through a tight U-turn. Several other animals moved aside as he led the farm's matriarch through the corral and into the dark interior of the barn; there he spoke softly to other bulky forms that I could hardly make out, and they too shifted to make room.

I have worked on a dairy farm myself, but I had never seen anyone handle animals so well. He talked in a gentle and personal way to each one, getting just the response he wanted. His cows were obviously part of Ed Kikendall's family, part of his heritage, and part of his satisfaction in life.

Still, he loves the forest as much as the farm, I learned. He worked part time for many years for the Forest Service, and helped to mark the famed Pacific Crest Trail that takes hikers through the high Cascades. He talked about the mountains, the lakes, the great snow-fields, and the stirring stands of mixed evergreens with obvious affection and a deep respect.

Over coffee I discussed with him and his wife, Hazel, the skills that make a farm function and that enrich country life. Mrs. Kikendall is as versatile as any farmer's wife of an earlier day. She cooks and bakes and preserves the products of the homestead, maintains vegetable and flower gardens, sews and knits and makes handsome quilts and rugs.

"We're never without homegrown vegetables," she said. "By the time the fresh ones are gone, I've canned enough to last the rest of the year."

One colorful example of her needle-work was a tapestry that hung on the living room wall; it intrigued me because its pictorial design was unlike any I had seen before. She had made it for the annual Grange Fair, to depict life in and around Winthrop. "This community has meant a lot to us," she said, "and this was my salute to it."

The Kikendalls' six children and 13 grandchildren all live in the Pacific Northwest, so family reunions at the farm occur often. As I was leaving I thought about such homecomings, and about the 50 years the Kikendalls have lived in this place, and about the tapestry with its technique of fine stitchery in a time-honored tradition.

The best of the old ways, I told myself, do not die, and especially in the mountains, where people seem to have an extra measure of appreciation for the past. Perhaps this is true in a particular way in the Far West, settled much later than the Appalachians, and the Ozarks. Many western families are only one or two generations removed from the region's first pioneers.

In much of the western mountain country the opportunists have come and gone, taking the wealth of furs, minerals, and timber with them. It is the patient people who remain; steady and independent, they seem to care little for wealth, and see no lasting gain in the pace that exploitation demands. They do not have much money; but as Len Blondell says, "You sort of string out your needs according to the times."

They have that sound sense of priorities, of the relative importance of things. "There's always another day," they say — because they are wise, not because they are lazy. The mountain way of life is rugged and demanding in terms of physical work and endurance; shelter and food are not easily assured where slopes are steep and snow covers the ground a good part of the year.

Yet there is something about the mountains that Glen Young and George Wright have found, that Ed and Hazel Kikendall understand, and that Leonard and Corky James are determined to pursue.

It has to do with space, and time, and peace, and soul. It is there — for those who want it enough. □

Born in Kansas City, Missouri, CLAY ANDERSON grew up on a farm in the Ozarks. After graduating from the University of Missouri School of Journalism, he served in the Army, then edited trade magazines in Chicago. In 1965 he returned to southern Missouri to become editor and owner of *The Ozarks Mountaineer*, a regional magazine.

National Geographic photographer BRUCE DALE, an Ohio native, has been on the Society's staff since 1964. His assignments have included the Ozarks and the Cumberland Gap for the magazine, and the world of the gypsies for Special Publications. He was named 1967 Magazine Photographer of the Year in the annual National Press Photographers Association competition.

CHARLTON OGBURN, reared in New York City and graduated from Harvard, worked for the State Department from 1946 to 1957. His nine books, chiefly on environmental subjects, include *The Winter Beach* and *The Continent in Our Hands*. He contributed the population chapter for the National Geographic Special Publication *As We Live and Breathe*.

After a boyhood spent in Minnesota, BILL PETERSON earned an M.S. degree in journalism from Northwestern University. He has reported for *The Courier-Journal* of Louisville, Kentucky, since 1967. His study of Great Society programs in eastern Kentucky resulted in *Coaltown Revisited: An Appalachian Notebook*, published in 1972.

ZEKE SCHER left his home state of Virginia after graduating from Washington and Lee University and headed west. He worked for newspapers in Montana and Iowa before joining *The Denver Post* in 1952. On his present assignment he roams the Rocky Mountain region fulltime, reporting for the *Post* Sunday edition's *Empire Magazine*.

Montana-born STEPHEN WENNSTROM attended Oregon State University and the University of Oregon. He became program director of the Northwest Outward Bound School, then resigned to do free-lance writing and photography. His mountain-climbing pursuits have taken him to the Grand Tetons, the Sierra Nevada, and Mount McKinley.

Index

Boldface indicates illustrations; *italic* refers to picture captions.

Library of Congress CIP Data
Main entry under title:
American mountain people.
Various authors.
Bibliography: p.
1. United States—Description and travel—1960- 2. Mountains—United States. 3. United States—Social life and customs—1945- I. National Geographic Society, Washington, D. C., Special Publications Division.
E169.02.A653 917.3 73-829
ISBN 0-87044-126-4

Acknowledgments

The Special Publications Division is grateful to the individuals and organizations listed here for their generous cooperation and assistance:
Bancroft Library; Elizabeth Gilbert, Loyal Jones, and Harry Segedy, Berea College, Kentucky; California Historical Society; Church of Jesus Christ of Latter-Day Saints; Denver Public Library; John Fetterman; Gary C. Gillum; The Henry E. Huntington Library; Sam King; Terry Mangan, State Historical Society of Colorado; Charles McRaven; Vance Mosley; National Park Service; Kenneth Pettitt, California State Library; The Smithsonian Institution; U. S. Forest Service; West Virginia University Library; Darrell Wilsey.

Additional Reading

The reader may want to check the *National Geographic Index* for related articles, and to refer to the following books:
John C. Campbell, *The Southern Highlander and His Homeland;* Harry M. Caudill, *Night Comes to the Cumberlands;* Allen H. Eaton, *Handicrafts of the Southern Highlands;* Elisabeth L. Egenhoff, *The Elephant as They Saw It;* Harry Hansen, ed., *Colorado, A Guide to the Highest State;* A. R. Harding, *Ginseng and Other Medicinal Plants;* Joseph Henry Jackson, *Gold Rush Album;* Horace Kephart, *Our Southern Highlanders;* David Lavender, *The Rockies;* Bill Peterson, *Coaltown Revisited;* Vance Randolph, *Ozark Magic and Folklore;* David S. Walls and John B. Stephenson, eds., *Appalachia in the Sixties;* T. H. Watkins, *Gold and Silver in the West;* W. D. Weatherford and Earl D. C. Brewer, *Life and Religion in Southern Appalachia;* Jack E. Weller, *Yesterday's People.*

Composition for *American Mountain People* by National Geographic's Phototypographic Division, Carl M. Shrader, Chief; Lawrence F. Ludwig, Assistant Chief. Printed and bound by Fawcett Printing Corp., Rockville, Md. Color separations by Colorgraphics, Inc., Beltsville, Md.; Graphic Color Plate, Inc., Stamford, Conn.; The Lanman Company, Alexandria, Va.; McCall Printing Company, Charlotte, N.C.; and Progressive Color Corp., Rockville, Md.

CVMBERLAND

GRA

BUCKSKIN P